11th Joint ACL-ISO Workshop on Interoperable Semantic Annotation 2015

(ISA-11)

AA005264

Held at the 11th International Conference on Computational Semantics (IWCS 2015)

London, United Kingdom
14 April 2015

Editor:

H. Bunt

ISBN: 978-1-5108-0226-1

Printed from e-media with permission by:

Curran Associates, Inc.
57 Morehouse Lane
Red Hook, NY 12571

proceedings.com

Some format issues inherent in the e-media version may also appear in this print version.

Copyright© (2015) by the Association for Computational Linguistics
All rights reserved.

Printed by Curran Associates, Inc. (2015)

For permission requests, please contact the Association for Computational Linguistics
at the address below.

Association for Computational Linguistics
209 N. Eighth Street
Stroudsburg, Pennsylvania 18360

Phone: 1-570-476-8006
Fax: 1-570-476-0860

acl@aclweb.org

Additional copies of this publication are available from:

Curran Associates, Inc.
57 Morehouse Lane
Red Hook, NY 12571 USA
Phone: 845-758-0400
Fax: 845-758-2634
Email: curran@proceedings.com
Web: www.proceedings.com

Workshop Programme

08.45 -- 09:00 Registration

09:00 -- 09:10 Opening by Workshop Chair

09:15 – 09:45 Harry Bunt: *On the Principles of Interoperable Semantic Annotation*
09:45 -- 10:15 Kiyong Lee and Harry Bunt: *ISO 24617-6: Principles of semantic annotation; Discussion of comments from DIS ballot*
10:15 -- 10:45 Kiyong Lee: *The annotation of measure expressions in ISO standards*

10:45 – 11:15 Coffee break

11:15 -- 11:45 Elisabetta Jezek and Rossella Varvara: *Instrument subjects without Instrument role*
11:45 -- 12:15 Jérémy Trione, Frédéric Béchet, Benoit Favre and Alexis Nasr: *Rapid FrameNet annotation of spoken conversation transcripts*
12:15 -- 12:30 Steven Neale, João Silva and António Branco: *An Accessible Interface Tool for Manual Word Sense Annotation*
12:30 -- 13:00 Julia Gil and James Pustejovsky: *The Semantics of Image Annotation*

13:00 – 14:00 Lunch break

14:00 -- 14:30 Ludivine Crible and Sandrine Zufferey: *Using a unified taxonomy to annotate discourse markers in speech and writing*
14:30 -- 15:00 Rashmi Prasad and Harry Bunt: *Semantic Relations in Discourse: The Current State of ISO 24617-8*
15:00 -- 15:20 Jet Hoek and Sandrine Zufferey: *Factors influencing implicitation of discourse relations across languages*

15:20 -- 15:50 Tea break

15:50 -- 16:20 Silvia Pareti: *Annotating Attribution Relations Across Languages and Genres*
16:20 -- 16:50 Hegler Tissot, Angus Roberts, Leon Derczynski, Genevieve Gorrell and Marcus Didonet Del Fabro: *Analysing Temporal Expressions Annotated in Clinical Notes*
16:50 -- 17:10 Volker Gast, Lennart Bierkandt and Christoph Rzymski: *Creating and retrieving tense and aspect annotations with GraphAnno, a lightweight tool for multilevel annotation*
17:10 -- 17:30 Kiyong Lee and Harry Bunt: Discussion of *possible new ISO projects in areas of semantic annotation*

17:30 Workshop Closing

Workshop Organizers/Organizing Committee

Harry Bunt	Tilburg University
Nancy Ide	Vassar College, Poughkeepsie, NY
Kiyong Lee	Korea University, Seoul
James Pustejovsky	Brandeis University, Waltham, MA
Laurent Romary	INRIA/Humboldt Universität Berlin

Workshop Programme Committee

Jan Alexandersson	DFKI, Saarbrücken
Harry Bunt	TiCC, Tilburg University
Nicoletta Calzolari	ILC-CNR, Pisa
Thierry Declerck	DFKI, Saarbrücken
Liesbeth Degand	Université Catholique de Louvain
Anna Esposito	Seconda Università di Napoli, Caserta
Alex Chengyu Fang	City University Hong Kong
Anette Frank	Universität Heidelberg
Robert Gaizauskas	University of Sheffield
Koiti Hasida	Tokyo University
Nancy Ide	Vassar College, Poughkeepsie
Daniel Hardt	Copenhagen Business Scool
Elisabetta Jezek	Università degli Studi di Pavia
Michael Kipp	University of Applied Sciences, Augsburg
Philippe Muller	IRIT, Université Paul Sabatier, Toulouse
Martha Palmer	University of Colorado, Boulder
Volha Petukhova	Universität des Saarlandes, Saarbrücken
Andrei Popescu-Belis	Idiap, Martigny, Switzerland
Rarhmi Prasad	University of Wisconsin, Milwaukee
Laurent Prévot	Aix-Marseille University
James Pustejovsky	Brandeis University
Laurent Romary	INRIA/Humboldt Universität Berlin
Ted Sanders	Universiteit Utrecht
Thorsten Trippel	University of Bielefeld
Piek Vossen	Vrije Universiteit Amsterdam
Bonnie Webber	School of Informatics, University of Edinburgh
Annie Zaenen	Stanford University

Proceedings Editor

Harry Bunt	Tilburg University

Table of contents

Author Index

On the principles of interoperable semantic annotation

Harry Bunt
TiCC, Tilburg Center for Cognition and Communication
Tilburg University, The Netherlands
harry.bunt@uvt.nl

Abstract

This paper summarizes the research that is leading to ISO standard 24617-6, which describes the approach to semantic annotation that characterizes the ISO semantic annotation framework (SemAF). It investigates the consequences and the risks of the SemAF strategy of developing separate annotation schemes for certain classes of semantic phenomena, with the long-term aim to combine these schemes into a single, wide- coverage scheme for semantic annotation. The principles are discussed for linguistic annotation in general and semantic annotation in particular that underly the SemAF effort. The notions of abstract syntax and concrete syntax are described with their relation to the specification of a metamodel and the semantics of annotations. Overlaps between the annotation schemes defined in SemAF parts are discussed, as well as semantic phenomena that cut across these schemes.

1 Introduction

ISO standard 24617-6, "Principles of semantic annotation", sets out the approach to semantic annotation that characterizes the ISO semantic annotation framework (SemAF). In addition, it provides guidelines for dealing with two issues regarding the annotation schemes defined in the different parts of SemAF: inconsistencies that may arise due to overlaps between annotation schemes, and semantic phenomena that cut across SemAF-parts, such as negation, modality, and quantification.

The purpose of ISO 24617-6 is to provide support for the establishment of a consistent and coherent set of international standards for semantic annotation. It does so in three ways. First, by making explicit which basic principles underly the approach followed in the SemAF parts that have already produced ISO standards (Part 1, Time and events; Part 2, Dialogue acts); and in the parts that are under way (Part 4, Semantic roles; Part 7, Spatial information; Part 8, Discourse relations). This approach lends methodological coherence to SemAF and helps to ensure consistency between existing, developing, and future SemAF parts. Second, by identifying overlaps between SemAF parts, and indicating how these may be dealt with. Third, by identifying common issues that cut across SemAF parts and which are not or only partially covered, where possible indicating directions for how these issues may be tackled.

Semantic annotation enhances primary data with information about their meaning. Given the current state of the art in semantics, it is unlikely that any existing formalism for representing semantic information would have general support from the research community. In practice, moreover, semantic annotation tasks often have the limited aim of annotating certain specific semantic phenomena, such as semantic roles, discourse relations, or coreference relations, rather than annotating the full meaning of primary data. Therefore a strategy was adopted to devise separate standards in different SemAF parts, with annotation schemes for specific semantic phenomena; over time, these schemes could develop into a wide-coverage framework for semantic annotation.

This 'crystal growth' strategy has proved fruitful in making progress in the establishment of standardized annotation concepts and schemes in support of the development of interoperable resources, but it also entails certain risks: (1) annotation schemes defined in different SemAF parts are not necessarily mutually consistent; (2) it may not be possible to combine the schemes, defined in different parts, into a coherent single scheme if they incorporate different views or employ different methodologies; and (3) some semantic phenomena are outside the scope of all SemAF parts but cannot be disregarded entirely in some parts, which may lead to unsatisfactory treatments of these phenomena. The methodological principles and guidelines provided in this standard are designed to minimize these risks.

Mutual consistency of SemAF parts is essential for making the integration possible of annotation schemes defined in different parts. Three aspects of consistency among annotation schemes can be distinguished:

- methodological consistency, i.e. the same approach is followed with respect to the distinction between abstract and concrete syntax and their interrelation, and with respect to their semantics;
- conceptual consistency, i.e. different schemes are based on compatible underlying views regarding their basic concepts, e.g. verbs are viewed as denoting states or events, rather than relations;
- terminological consistency, i.e. terms which occur in different annotation schemes have the same meaning in every scheme, and the same term is used across annotation schemes for indicating the same concept.

The rest of this paper is organized as follows. Section 2 summarizes certain principles for standard annotation schemes in general, and some that are specific for the annotation of semantic information. Section 3 outlines the methodological basis of SemAF, taking these principles into account. Section 4 discusses cases of overlaps between annotation schemes and the consistency issues that these give rise to. Section 5 discusses a number of semantic phenomena whose annotation cuts across SemAF parts. The paper ends with conclusions in Section 6.

2 Annotation principles and requirements

The ISO efforts aiming to develop standards for semantic annotation rest on a number of basic principles for semantic annotation, some of which have been laid out by Bunt & Romary (2002; 2004) and developed further in Bunt (2010; 2013); others have been formulated as general principles for linguistic annotation and are part of the ISO Linguistic Annotation Framework (LAF, ISO 24623:2012). The latter are often of a very general nature, such as the principle that segments of primary data are referred to in a uniform and TEI-compliant way, and the principle that the use of multiple layers over the primary data is supported, with stand-off annotation and a uniform way of cross-referencing between layers.

The use of layers of annotation is of particular relevance for SemAF because it allows different layers to be used for different types of semantic information, such as one layer for the annotation of events, time and space, and another one for semantic roles, each with their own annotation scheme. While this allows in principle the use of layers which are not mutually consistent, the 'crystal growth' strategy of SemAF is designed to allow the annotation schemes for the various types of semantic information to grow into a single coherent annotation scheme.

Of particular relevance for SemAF is also the distinction between 'annotations' and 'representations' (Ide & Romary, 2004). An annotation is any item of linguistic information that is added to primary data, independent of a particular representation format. A representation is a rendering of an annotation in a particular format, e.g. as an XML expression. This distinction has incited the development of a methodology for developing semantic annotation schemes with an 'abstract syntax' of annotations and a 'concrete syntax' of representations. This methodology is described in Section 3.

Other general principles for designing annotation schemes include empirical validity; theoretical justification; learnability for humans and machines; generalizability; completeness; and compatibility with existing good practices. Of special importance are moreover the requirements of extensibility and variable granularity:

Extensibility ISO standard annotation schemes are designed to be language-, domain- and application-independent, but some applications or some languages may require specific concepts which are not relevant in other applications or languages. Therefore, annotation schemes should allow extension with language-, domain-, or application-specific concepts.

Variable granularity One way to achieve good coverage is to include annotation concepts of a high level of generality, which cover many specific instances. Since an annotation scheme which uses only very general concepts would not be optimally useful, this leads to the principle that annotation schemes should include concepts with different levels of granularity. This is also beneficial for its interoperability, as it gives more possibilities for conversion to and from existing annotation schemes and the standard scheme.

The idea behind annotating a text, which dates from long before the digital era, is to add information to a primary text information in order to support its understanding. The semantic annotation of digital source text has a similar purpose, namely to support the understanding of the text by humans as well as by machines. Therefore, semantic annotations must satisfy the principle of 'semantic adequacy':

Semantic adequacy: semantic annotations add information to source data in a form that has a well-defined semantics, ensuring the annotations to be machine-interpretable.

3 The methodological basis of SemAF

3.1 Steps in the design of an annotation scheme

An annotation scheme determines which information may be added to primary data, and how that information is expressed. When an annotation scheme is designed from scratch, the first step to take is a conceptual analysis of the information that annotations should capture. This analysis identifies the concepts that form the building blocks of annotations, and specifies how these blocks may be used to build annotation structures. This step corresponds to what is known in ISO projects as the establishment of a 'metamodel', i.e. the expression of a conceptual view of the information in annotatations. The second step, indicated by '2' in Figure 1, articulates this conceptual view as a formal specification of categories of entities and relations, and of how annotation structures can be built up from elements in these categories. This formal specification defines the *'abstract syntax'* of an annotation language.

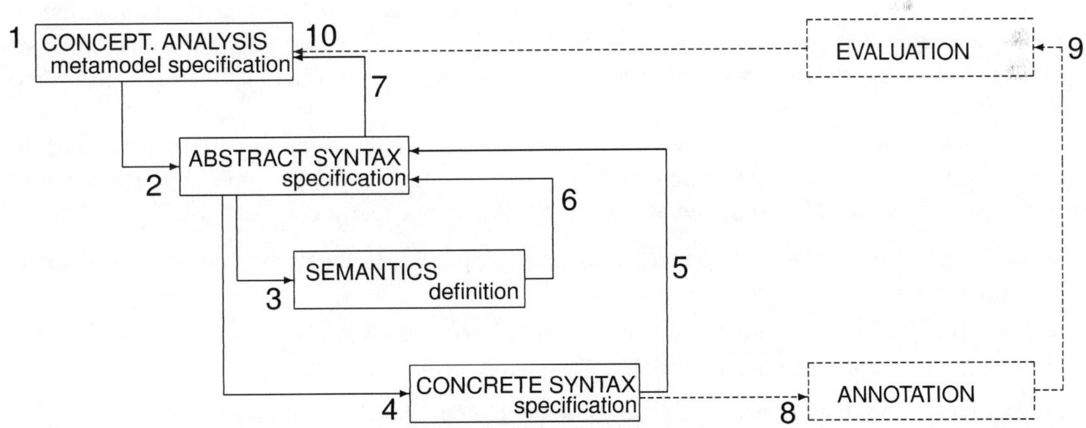

Figure 1: Steps and feedback loops in the CASCADES method

While these two steps make explicit what information can be captured in annotations, they do not specify how annotations should be represented, for example as XML strings, as logical formulas, as graphs, as feature structures, or otherwise; the abstract syntax defines the specification of information in terms of set-theoretic structures. The definition of a representation format for annotation structures occurs in step 4 in Figure 1, the specification of a concrete syntax.

Step 3 is the specification of the meaning of the structures defined by the abstract syntax, i.e. the specification of a semantics for annotation structures. By definition, a representation defined by the concrete syntax has the meaning of the abstract annotation structure that it represents.

This method for designing an annotation scheme is called CASCADES: **C**onceptual analysis, **A**bstract syntax, **S**emantics, and **C**oncrete syntax for **A**nnotation language **DES**ign. Figure 1 visualizes the CASCADES method, of which the central concept of an abstract syntax for annotations with the specification of a semantics, was introduced in Bunt (2010). The dotted parts of Figure 1 are discussed in Section 3.3.

The CASCADES method is useful for enabling a systematic design process, in which due attention is given to the conceptual and semantic choices on which more superficial decisions such as the choice of particular XML attributes and values should be based. Apart from supporting the design of an annotation scheme from scratch, this method also provides support for improving an existing annotation scheme. This support consists not only in the distinction of four well-defined design steps but also of procedures and guidelines for taking these steps and using feedback loops, as discussed in Section 3.3.

3.2 Metamodels, abstract syntax, concrete syntax, and semantics

A metamodel of an annotation scheme is a schematic representation of the relations between the concepts that are used in annotations. Over the years, two slightly different notions of a metamodel have been used in ISO projects, namely: (a) as a representation of the relations between the most important concepts that are mentioned in the document in which the standard is proposed; (b) as a representation of the relations between the concepts denoted by terms that occur in annotations. Metamodels of type (a) may be helpful for nontechnical readers to better understand an annotation scheme; those of type (b) are a visualization of the abstract syntax of the scheme, and are helpful to see at a glance what information the annotations may contain. Note that a type (a) metamodel may have a type (b) metamodel as a proper part.

The abstract syntax of an annotation scheme specifies the information in annotations in terms of set-theoretical structures such as the triple $\langle e_1, e_2, R_i \rangle$ which relates the two arguments e_1 and e_2 through the relation R_i. More generally, these structures are n-tuples of elements which are either basic concepts, taken from a store of basic concepts called the 'conceptual inventory' of the abstract syntax specification, or n-tuples of such structures. An *annotation structure* is a set of *entity structures*, which contain semantic information about a region of primary data, and *link structures*, which describe a semantic relation between two such regions.

A concrete syntax specifies a representation format for annotation structures, such as the representation of a triple like $\langle e_1, e_2, R_i \rangle$ by a list of three XML elements, of which the element <srLink event="#e1" participant="#x1" semRole="agent"/> represents the relation and the other two elements represent two entity structures.

A representation format for annotation structures should ideally give an exact expression of the information contained in annotation structures. A concrete syntax, defining a representation format for a given abstract syntax, is said to be *ideal* if it has the following properties:

- Completeness: every annotation structure defined by the abstract syntax can be represented by an expression defined by the concrete syntax;
- Unambiguity: every representation defined by the concrete syntax is the rendering of exactly one annotation structure defined by the abstract syntax.

The representation format defined by an ideal concrete syntax is called an *ideal representation format*. Due to its completeness, an ideal concrete syntax defines a function from annotation structures to representations, and due to its unambiguity there is also an inverse function from representations to annotation structures. It follows that for any two ideal representation formats are interoperable: there is a complete meaning-preserving mapping from one format to the other. Figure 2 visualizes the relations between abstract syntax, semantics, and multiple ideal concrete syntactic specifications.

An ideal concrete syntax can be derived systematically from an abstract syntax. For example, a concrete syntax defining XML representations can be constructed as follows:

1. For each element of the conceptual inventory specify an XML name;
2. For each type of entity structure $\langle m, s \rangle$ define an XML element with the following attributes and values:

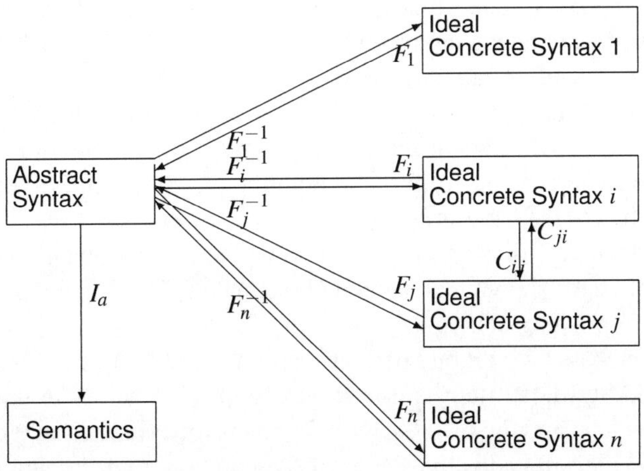

Figure 2: Relations Relations between abstract syntax, semantics, and concrete syntax of annotations.

- the special attribute 'xml:id', whose value is an identifier of the element;
- the special attribute 'target', whose value represents the markable *m*;
- attributes whose values represent the components of *s*.

3. For each type of link structure define an XML element with three attributes, whose values refer to the representations of the linked entity structures and to the relation that links them.

Bunt (2011) proposes to provide a semantics based on Discourse Representation Theory (DRT, Kamp & Reyle, 1993). The use of Discourse Representation Structure (DRSs) has an advantage over the use of first-order logic, with which DRSs are formally equivalent, since DRSs were designed to facilitate incremental construction. This can be exploited when constructing DRSs systematically from the components of an annotation representation.

The CASCADES approach defines a semantics for abstract annotation structures. Such a semantics can exploit the fact that entity structures and link structures are n-tuples of semantic concepts, the significance of an element in being encoded by its position. Bunt (2014) shows how annotation structures can be translated into DRSs in a compositional way, combining the translations of the component entity structures and link structures.

3.3 Steps forward and feedback in the design process

While the procedures for making the CASCADES steps are helpful for defining well-founded annotation schemes, it would be unrealistic to think that annotation schemes can be designed simply through a linear sequence of steps, from conceptual analysis to the specification of a representation format. Realistic design processes require feedback loops.

Pustejovsky and colleagues have introduced the 'MAMA' cycle for developing an annotation scheme (see Moszkowicz, 2012; Pustejovsky and Stubbs, 2012) , which distinguishes four steps: (1) Model; (2) Annotate; (3) Evaluate; and (4) Revise. In step (1) an annotation scheme is constructed, which can subsequently be revised and improved by repeating the cycle <2,3,4,1> until the scheme is stable.

In the CASCADES method, feedback cycles can occur between each of the four design stages, as shown in Figure 1. The feedback cycle <5;4> is especially useful when combined with the 'inner cycle <3;6>, to form the iterative feedback loop <5;<3;6>*;4>. This feedback loop is central to the application of the CASCADES method for improving an existing representation format, for detecting and resolving semantic deficiencies, or for turning an existing format into an annotation scheme that meets the requirements of the ISO Linguistic Annotation Framework and the requirement of semantic adequacy. In practice, the design of semantic annotations mostly starts from an existing representation format. An abstract syntax (with a semantics) can then be constructed that fits the representations and meets the LAF requirements and the requirement of semantic adequacy by following the iterative feedback loop <5;<3;6>*;4 >, commencing with the reconstruction of an abstract syntax.

The CASCADES method has been used in this 'reverse engineering' mode in the development of ISO-TimeML (ISO 24617-1), starting from TimeML, and in preliminary studies for the definition of an ISO standard for discourse relation annotation starting from the annotations in the Penn Discourse Treebank (PDTB) (see Bunt, Prasad & Joshi, 2012). Ide et al. (2011) have 'reverse-engineered' an abstract syntax for the PDTB representation format with the aim of designing a GrAF representation (Ide & Suderman, 2001) for these annotations, and have shown that, even without specifying a semantics for this abstract syntax, this leads to significant improvements.

The CASCADES design steps and feedback loops integrate perfectly with the MAMA development cycles, as shown in Figure 1, viewing the CASCADES steps and feedback loops together as an implementation of the Model stage of the MAMA cycle, and the CASCADES feedback loops as an implementation of the Revise stage, to which the MAMA cycle adds the stages of 'Annotation' and 'Evaluation' in between the CASCADES stages of Concrete Syntax specification and Conceptual Analysis. This integration clarifies the relation between the Model and Revise stages in the MAMA cycle. Intuitively, revising an existing annotation scheme should involve some of the same activities as the Model stage; the CASCADES steps make this explicit, since the feedback loops for revising an annotation scheme are also part of the modelling stage.

3.4 Optional elements in an annotation scheme

The abstract - concrete syntax distinction opens up interesting possibilities for optional elements in annotations and their representations

In a given annotation task it may be relevant to take information into account which does not form part of the focus of the annotation scheme but which may be useful for performing the task. For example, in coreference annotation it is useful to identify the noun phrases that are potential antecedents of referential pronouns according to their grammatical number and their grammatical or natural gender, depending on which of these properties is relevant in the grammar of the language under consideration. It is therefore useful to annotate the number and gender of noun phrases and pronouns. This may now be supported by an annotation scheme which includes the representation of gender and number in the concrete syntax but does not include this information in the abstract syntax, and therefore does not deal with the semantics of number of gender annotations.

Another form of optionality is that the concrete syntax defines default values for certain attributes. For example, an attribute 'polarity', with possible values "positive" and "negative", can be assumed to have the value "positive" by default. Optional components of this kind do correspond to elements in the abstract syntax, and do have a semantics.

A third kind of optionality is when semantic information may take more or less elaborate forms. An example is the annotation of attribution and argument type for discourse relations. In an explorative study which applies the CASCADES method to re-engineer the annotation scheme of the Penn Discourse Treebank (see Bunt, Prasad & Joshi, 2012) the entity structures that annotate arguments of discourse relations are defined as follows: *"An Argument Entity Structure is a pair $\langle m, s \rangle$ consisting of a markable m and the semantic information s, which is either vacuous (i.e. the entity structure only identifies the markable corresponding to an argument of a discourse relation), or contains information about the attribution of the argument and/or specifies the type of the argument."* Allowing the semantic information in these entity structures to be vacuous is a way of saying that the semantic information does not have to include certain components. This form of optionality is useful for dealing with information which is not always applicable or is irrelevant in certain cases.

3.5 Theory, practice and evaluation of annotation schemes

The CASCADES method of designing an annotation scheme can be viewed as a *theory* of annotation scheme design. Two ideas are central to this theory:

- annotations mean something; they are not just labels or XML strings that can mean whatever someone would like them to mean;[1]
- the choice of particular tag names and tag structures is of secondary importance; of primary importance is the determination of concepts and conceptual structures which the annotation scheme allows to be represented.

The CASCADES theory thus offers a way of evaluating the 'soundness' of an annotation scheme, namely the extent to which its representations are complete and unambiguous. Extended with the MAMA steps of Annotation and Evaluation, it moreover offers the steps for evaluating the empirical validity of an annotation scheme and for combining the feedback from an empirical evaluation with that of revising the annotation scheme in a theoretically sound way.

For practical purposes, if a certain annotation task calls for terminological and conceptual deviations from an existing annotation scheme, it may be sufficient to check that there is a mapping between the two sets of terms and between the respective representation structures. If a conceptual deviation is in fact a conceptual *extension*, the of course such mapping will fully work in one direction only.

4 Overlaps between annotation schemes

4.1 Spatial and temporal relations as semantic roles

The annotation schemes of ISO-TimeML (ISO 24617-1) and ISOspace (ISO 24617-7) include relations between events and their place and time of occurrence, as well as relations between temporal and spatial entities. The annotation scheme of SemAF-SR (ISO 24617-4) views semantic roles as relations between events and their participants, including spatial and temporal participants.

SemAF-SR defines the following eight semantic roles of a spatial or temporal character: (1) Location; (2) Initial-location; (3) Final-location; (4) Path; (5) Distance; (6) Duration; (7) Initial-time; and (8) Final-time. These concepts also occur in ISOspace or in ISO-TimeML, sometimes using exactly the same terms. For example, ISOspace defines a 'path' as a 'series of locations', like a road or a river, which can be used to get from one location to another. ISOspace is inconsistent in this respect with SemAF-SR, which defines Path as *Intermediate location or trajectory between two locations, or in a designated space, where an event occurs*, and thus views a path as inherently related to an event. So whereas 'path' is a spatial object in ISOspace, it is a relational notion in SemAF-SR.

ISOspace also defines 'event-path' as the dynamic notion of a trajectory followed in a motion, which is in essence the same concept as the semantic role Path in SemAF-SR. There is, on the other hand a difference between the way ISOspace views an event-path and the way SemAF-SR views a Path role, since the latter is a *relation* whereas the ISOspace notion is a *spatial object*.

A general question is whether all the distinctions among spatial and temporal relations that are made in ISOspace and ISO-TimeML should be reflected in distinctions between semantic roles in SemAF-SR. For example, ISOspace uses the attribute 'goalReached', with possible values "true", "false" and 'uncertain", in order to distinguish between cases like *John arrived in Boston*, where John reached his destination, from *John left for Boston*, where we don't know if he did. SemAF-SR so far has no provisions for making this distinction.

[1] An exception is the case of an instance of the second kind of optionality, discussed in Section 3.4, which does not have a semantics.

4.2 Events

Events take central stage both in ISO-TimeML and in ISOspace. For the sake of consistency, ISOspace inherits the typology of events defined in ISO-TimeML. On the other hand, ISOspace makes a basic distinction between motion events and non-motion events that cuts through the ISO-TimeML typology; whether this can lead to consistency problems needs to be investigated. Events are also of central importance in SemAF-SR, which views semantic roles as relations between events and their participants, but does not assume any particular typology of events.

The ISOspace distinction between motion events and non-motion events does seem relevant for semantic role assigment, since only motion verbs have spatial entities in roles like Initial Location, Path, and Final Location. Motion verbs used in a negative sentence, such as *John did not leave home* seem to require a different spatial role for characterizing the relation between *leave* and *home*, which is not available in ISO-SR. The same is true for *John stayed at home*.

4.3 Discourse relations in dialogue

The study of semantic relations in discourse is very much focused on the intersentential relations that lend coherence to a text; however, these relations may occur also in dialogue, not only within but also between speaker turns (see e.g. Tonelli et al., 2010; Petukhova et al., 2011; Lascarides & Asher, 2007). The ISO 24617-2 annotation scheme for dialogue act annotation therefore includes the concept of a 'rhetorical relation', however, it leaves open which specific relations may be used in dialogue annotation, recommending annotators to use the relations defined in the forthcoming standard ISO 24617-8 This is a good example of how the annotation schemes of different SemAF parts can be combined.

Utterances in dialogue may also be related by other semantic relations than those that are found in written text. The ISO dialogue act annotation scheme defines two other relations: (1) 'feedback dependence', which occurs when a dialogue act provides or elicits feedback about the success of processing (recognizing, understanding, or accepting) one or more previous dialogue acts – the 'scope' of the feedback act; and (2) 'functional dependence', for dialogue acts that due to their communicative function depend for their semantic content on a preceding dialogue act, such as an answer being dependent on a question. These relations are not present in any existing annotation scheme for discourse relations, presumably because of their focus on written discourse. The ISO annotation scheme for discourse relations inherits these relations from the ISO-24617-2 scheme.

5 Ubiquitous semantic phenomena

5.1 Quantification

Quantification phenomena arise whenever a predicate is applied to one or more sets of individuals, as in *Three men moved both pianos*. Quantification has been studied extensively, but not so much in relation to events, times and places. Still, in principle any relation between two sets of entities is quantified, as are the relations between events and temporal entities, for instance by means of temporal quantifiers such as *always, sometimes, every Monday*. For this reason, ISO-TimeML has some provisions for time-related quantification. The attribute 'quant' has been introduced for this purpose as one of the attributes of temporal entities.

Quantification cannot be analysed satisfactorily by means of attributes of temporal entities, however, since quantification phenomena are not properties of the entities participating in a predication, but are aspects of relations, as the following example illustrates, where three men are involved collectively in moving a piano and individually in drinking a beer.

(1) The three men had a beer before moving the piano.

An analysis of quantification in terms of feature structures has been proposed by Bunt (2005; 2013b) which can be the basis for annotating quantification in such a way that components of annotation structures correspond to the linguistic expression of quantification. This supports a semantic interpretation that can be combined with a compositional semantics of noun phrases, which is useful since many of the features of quantifications are expressed syntactically in noun phrases. The semantic adequacy of the proposal is demonstrated by a systematic translation of annotation structures into discourse representation structures.

5.2 Quantities and measures

Duration, length, volume, weight, price, and many other ways of measuring quantities of something are linguistically expressed by means of a unit of measurement plus a numerical indication, such as *one and a half hour, 90 minutes, just over two kilos*. Semantically, a measure is an equivalence class formed by pairs $\langle n, u\rangle$ where n is a numerical predicate and u is a unit (Bunt, 1985). Given the relations between the units in a particular system of units, like 1 hour = 60 minutes, any of the equivalent pairs can serve as a representative of the class. Units can be complex, like kilowatt-hour or meter per second. Formally, a unit is either a basic unit or a triple $\langle u_1, u_2, Q\rangle$ where $Q = \times$ (multiplication) or $Q = /$ (division) and u_1 and u_2 are (possibly complex) units.

The abstract syntax of annotations for quantities can be defined by introducing pairs $\langle n, u\rangle$, where u is either an elementary unit or a triple, as indicated above. A corresponding XML-based concrete syntax uses an element 'amount' with attribute-value pairs for the numerical part and the unit part, as in the following representation of *three miles*:

(2) <amount xml:id="a1" target="#m1" num="3" unit="mile"/>

ISOspace includes amounts of space for measuring distances; ISO-TimeML includes amounts of time for measuring durations. In both cases, only elementary units are considered; the above approach can be used to generalize this for units of velocity, for example, as illustrated in the following representation of *sixty miles per hour*:

(3) <amount xml:id="am1" target="#m1" num="60" unit="#u1"/>
<unit xml:id="u1" target="#m2" unit1="mile" unit2="hour" operation="division"/>

Amount expressions involving comparisons, as in *We walked more than five miles*, may be treated as involving an existential quantification over locations, as: *There is an amount of space greater than 5 miles that we walked*:

(4) <event xml:id="e1" target="#m2" pred="walk"/>
<entity xml:id="x1" target="#m1"/>
<srLxink event="#e1" participant="#x1" roleType="agent"/>
<amount xml:id="d1" target="#m3"/>
<amount xml_id="d2" target="#m4" num="5" unit="mile"/>
<relation arg1="#d1" arg2="#d2" relType="greaterThen"/>
<srLink event="#e1" participant="#d1" roleType="distance"/>

5.3 Negation, modality, factuality, and attribution

Negation, modality, factuality and attribution are different but related aspects of the factual content of an utterance or a text. Consider the following example from the Penn Discourse Treebank:

(5) "The public is buying the market when in reality there is plenty of grain to be shipped", said Bill Biederman, Allendale Inc. director.

Even though Biedermann says *"in reality"*, it would be incorrect to conclude from this text that there is plenty of grain to be shipped. The source to which a statement is attributed is crucial to take into account: if the Wall Street Journal would report directly(rather than quote somebody) that there is plenty of grain to be shipped, then it would probably be more justified to draw this conclusion.

Negations evidently also have a strong influence on which information can be extracted from a text. ISO-TimeML makes use of an attribute 'polarity', with possible values "positive" and 'negative", as one of the attributes of an event. Positive and negative are just two extremes or a scale of possibilities, however. Modalities as expressed by *probably, maybe* and *surely*, as well as the attribution of the claim to a certain source, all have an influence on the possibilities of extracting factual information from a text. Expressions of modality have been studied by Karttunen (1971; 2012). The factuality of statements about events has been studied by Sauri (2008) and annotated in the FactBank (Sauri & Pustejovsky, 2009). See also Morante & Daelemans (2011) and Pareti (2012; 2015) for work on the annotation of negation, modality and attribution.

5.4 Modification and qualification

5.4.1 Nominal modification

The modification of nominal expressions, e.g. by adjectives, prepositional phrases, or relative clauses, gives rise to many of the same issues as the expression of quantification; in particular, issues of scope and distribution arise in much the same way. Consider the following example of a text next to a box of bell peppers:

(6) Bell peppers for fifty pesos

This is ambiguous as to whether *for fifty pesos* applies to the individual bell peppers in the box or to the whole lot (collective reading). Adjectives and prepositional phrases, used as modifiers, can be viewed as one-place predicates, whose application to a set of arguments gives rise to quantificational issues, as noted in Section 4.1. The ambiguity of (6) is due to an ambiguity in the way the predicate is applied to its arguments. This suggests an approach to the annotation of modification in terms of annotation structures that consist of a predicate, a set of arguments, and the type of relation between them (such as the 'restrictive modifier' relation type). Such a structure allows the distribution of the modification to be a property of the relation type. In an XML representation, such an annotation could look as follows:

(7) a. heavy boxes
b. <entity id="x1" target="#m2" signature="set"/>
<property id="p1" target="#m1 />
<modLink id="m1" head="#x1" modifier="#p1" relType="restrModifier" distribution="individual"/>

Modification by means of relative clauses gives rise to all the issues that are known to arise in quantifications, as can be seen by transforming a quantified sentence into a modified noun phrase – see the sentence pairs (8) and (9):

(8) a. That crane moved thirty big pipes.
b. Thirty big pipes moved by that crane.

(9) a. Two students read the six papers.
b. The six papers read by two students.

Sentence (8b) has the same ambiguity as (8a) in the distributive aspect of the quantification, i.e. whether the crane moved the pipes one by one or all in one go. Similarly, (9b) has the same ambiguity as (9a) with respect to the scopes of the quantifications.

In view of the analogy between modification and quantification, it seems commendable to develop an approach to the annotation of modification integrated with that of quantification.

5.4.2 Qualification

The notion of a 'qualifier' has been introduced in ISO 24617-2 in order to make more subtle distinctions between dialogue act types then would be possible by just using the set of communicative functions defined in the annotation scheme. Although this set is fairly comprehensive, it is not sufficient for dealing with subtle differences like those in (10).

(10) A: Would you like to have some coffee?
a. B: Only if you have it ready.
b. B: Maybe; how much time do we have?
c. B: Maybe later
d. B: Coffee, wonderful!
e. B: Coffee? At midnight??

These examples show the conditional acceptance of an offer (a); an uncertain acceptance (b); an uncertain rejection (c); an acceptance with pleasure (d); and a rejection with surprise (e). In order to take such modalities into account, which can occur with every dialogue act that has a responsive character, Petukhova and Bunt (2010) proposed the use of qualifiers for certainty, conditionality, and sentiment. These are optional elements in the abstract syntax of dialogue act annotations, which means that they do not have to be used, but if they are, then they have a semantic interpretation.

Qualifiers may be an interesting addition in other SemAF-parts as well, such as in the annotation of semantic roles. For example, the Agent role is defined in SemAF-SR as the involvement of *a participant who acts intentionally or consciously*. So when annotating a sentence like *Peter dropped his plate on the kitchen floor* the question arises whether this was done intentionally or not. If it was, then this could be made explicit by means of a intentionality qualifier. Similarly for discourse relation annotation, in examples like *but unexpectedly, but perhaps*, or *but fortunately* in order to annotate not just a contrastive relation but also the speaker's certainty or sentiment .about what happened, contrary to expectation.

6 Conclusions and future work

Efforts that aim to improve the interoperability of semantically annotated resources, taking place under the umbrella of the ISO Semantic Annotation Framework (SemAF), have as their most important characteristic the use of an abstract syntax underlying concrete annotation representations and the specification of a semantics of annotation structures. The importance of this approach is that it ensures that any two representation formats which have 'complete' expressive power and are 'unambiguous', are semantically interoperable: representations in one format can be converted to those in the other. We have also shown that this approach opens interesting alternative possibilities for the use of optional elements in semantic annotations.

In this paper we have identified various semantic phenomena that cut across SemAF annotation schemes for semantic roles, for time and space, for events, for discourse relations and for dialogue acts; for some of these phenomena (such as quantification and nominal modification) we have indicated promising directions for how they may be dealt with. Together with the analysis given in this paper of the overlaps between SemAF annotation schemes, this contributes to an agenda for future work that aims at the establishment of powerful annotation schemes for interoperable semantic annotation.

References

Asher, N. (1993). *Reference to abstract objects in discourse.* Dordrecht: Kluwer.

Bunt, H. (1985). *Mass Terms and Model-Theoretic Semantics.* Cambridge University Press.

Bunt, H. (2005). Quantification and Modification Represented as Feature Structures. In *Proceedings 6th International Workshop on Computational Semantics (IWCS-6)*, Tilburg, Netherlands, pp. 54–65.

Bunt, H. (2010). A methodology for designing semantic annotation languages exploring semantic-syntactic ISO-morphisms. In *Proceedings of the Second International Conference on Global Interoperability for Language Resources (ICGL 2010)*, Hong Kong: City University, pp. 29–46.

Bunt, H. (2013). A methodology for designing semantic annotations. TiCC Technical Report TR 2013-001, Tilburg University.

Bunt, H. (2013b). *The annotation of quantification and its interpretation.* University of Potsdam.

Bunt, H. (2014). Annotations that effectively contribute to semantic interpretation. In H. Bunt, J. Bos, and S. Pulman (Eds.), *Computing Meaning, Vol. 4*, pp. 49–70. Dordrecht: Springer.

Bunt, H., R. Prasad, and A. Joshi (2012). First steps toward an ISO standard for the annotation of discourse relations. In *Proceedings 7th Joint ACL-ISO Workshop on Interoperable Semantic Annotation (ISA-7), Istanbul*, Paris: ELRA, pp. 60–69.

Bunt, H. and J. Pustejovsky (2010). Annotating temporal and event quantification. In *Proceedings 5th Joint ACL-ISO Workshop on Interoperable Semantic Annotation (ISA-5)*, Hong Kong: City University, pp. 15–22.

Bunt, H. and L. Romary (2002). Towards Multimodal Content Representation. In K. S. Choi (Ed.), *Proceedings of LREC 2002, Workshop on International Standards of Terminology and Language Resources Management*, Las Palmas, pp. 54–60. Paris: ELRA.

Bunt, H. and L. Romary (2004). Standardization in Multimodal Content Representation: Some methodological issues. In *Proceedings of LREC 2004*, Lisbon, pp. 2219–2222. Paris: ELRA.

Hovy, E. and E. Maier (1992). *Parsimonious or profligate: how many and which discourse structure relations? ISI research report.* Marina del Rey: Information Sciences Institute, University of Southern California.

Ide, N. and H. Bunt (2010). Anatomy of annotation schemes: Mapping to GrAF. In *Proceedings 4th Linguistic Annotation Workshop (LAW IV)*, Uppsala.

Ide, N. and L. Romary (2004). International Standard for a Linguistic Annotation Framework. *Natural Language Engineering 10*, 211–225.

ISO (2012a). *ISO 24617-1: 2012, Language Resource Management - Semantic Annotation Framework (SemAF) - Part 1: Time and events.* Geneva: ISO.

ISO (2012b). *ISO 24617-2:2012, Language Resource Management - Semantic Annotation Framework (SemAF) - Part 2: Dialogue acts.* Geneva: ISO.

ISO (2014a). *ISO 24617-4: 2014, Language Resource Management - Semantic Annotation Framework (SemAF) - Part 4: Semantic roles.* Geneva: ISO.

ISO (2014b). *ISO 24617-7: 2014, Language Resource Management - Semantic Annotation Framework (SemAF) - Part 7: Spatial information.* Geneva: ISO.

ISO (2015a). *ISO 24617-6:2015, Language Resource Management - Semantic Annotation Framework (SemAF) - Part 6: Principles of semantic annotation.* Geneva: ISO.

ISO (2015b). *ISO CD 24617-8:2015, Language Resource Management - Semantic Annotation Framework (SemAF) - Part 8: Semantic relations in discourse.* Geneva: ISO.

Kamp, H. and U. Reyle (1993). *From Discourse to Logic.* Dordrecht: Kluwer Academic Publishers.

Karttunen, L. (1971). Implicative verbs. *Language 47*, 340–358.

Karttunen, L. (2012). Simple and phrasal implicatives. In *Proceedings of SEM 2012*, Montreal, pp. 124–131. Association for Computational Linguistics.

Lascarides, A. and N. Asher (2007). Segmented discourse representation theory: Dynamic semantics with discoure structure. In H. Bunt and R. Muskens (Eds.), *Computing Meaning, Vol. 3*, pp. 87–124. Dordrecht: Springer.

Morante, R. and W. Daelemans (2011). Annotating modality and negation for a machine learning evaluation. In *CLEF 2011 Labs and Workshop, Notebook Papers.*

Pareti, S. (2012). The independent encoding of attribution relations. In *Proceedings 8th Joint ACL ? ISO Workshop on Interoperable Semantic Annotation (ISA-8, "ISA in Pisa")*, Pisa, pp. 48–55.

Pareti, S. (2015). Annotating attribution relations across languages and genres. In *Proceedings 11th Joint ACL ? ISO Workshop on Interoperable Semantic Annotation (ISA-11)*, London.

Petukhova, V. and H. Bunt (2010). Introducing communicative function qualifiers. In *Proceedings Second International Conference on Global Interoperability for Language resources (ICGL-2), Hong Kong*, pp. 132 – 132.

Petukhova, V., L. Prévot, and H. Bunt (2011). Discourse relations in dialogue. In *Proceedings 6th Joint ACL - ISO Workshop on Interoperable Semantic Annotation (ISA-6)*, Oxford, pp. 18–27.

Prasad, R. and H. Bunt (2015). Semantic relations in discourse: The current state of ISO 24617-8. In *Proceedings 11th Joint ACL-ISO Workshop on Interoperable Semantic Annotation (ISA-11)*, pp. 80–92.

Prasad, R., N. Dinesh, A. Lee, E. Miltsakaki, L. Robaldo, A. Joshi, and B. Webber (2008). The Penn Discourse TreeBank 2.0. In *Proceedings 6th International Conference on Language Resources and Systems (LREC 2008)*, Marrakech.

Pustejovsky, J. and J. Moszkowics (2010). The role of model testing in standards development: The case of iso-space. In *Proceedings 8th International Conference on Language Resources and Evaluation(LREC 2012, Istanbul*. ELDA, Paris.

Pustejovsky, J. and A. Stubbs (2012). *Natural Language Annotation for Machine Learning*. O'Reilly.

Sauri, R. (2008). *A Factuality Profiler for Eventualities in Text.* Ph.D. Thesis, Brandeis University.

Sauri, R. and J.Pustejovsky (2009). Factbank: a corpus annotated with event factuality. *Journal of Language Resources and Evaluation 43 (3)*, 227–268.

Tonelli, S., G. Riccardi, R. Prasad, and A. Joshi (2010). Annotation of discourse relations for conversational spoken dialogs. In *Proceedings 7th International Conference on Language Resources and Systems (LREC 2010)*, Genoa.

Using a unified taxonomy to annotate discourse markers in speech and writing

CRIBLE Ludivine
Catholic University of Louvain (UCL)
ludivine.crible@uclouvain.be

ZUFFEREY Sandrine
University of Fribourg
sandrine.zufferey@unifr.ch

Abstract

We report an annotation experiment aiming at assessing the use of a single functional taxonomy of sense relations for discourse markers in spoken and written data. We start by presenting an operational definition of the category of DMs and its application to identify tokens of DMs in corpora. We then present an original annotation experiment making use of a unified taxonomy to annotate written and spoken data in English and French. In this experiment, we test the reliability of the annotations made separately by two annotators and the applicability of the tag set across two languages in the spoken and written modes. Our experiment leads us to conclude that: i) spoken data is not more difficult to annotate than written data in terms of inter-annotator agreement, ii) recurrent problems are found across the two languages and modes, iii) the reliability of the annotation scheme is improved by the use of more explicit instructions and training.

1 Introduction

Discourse markers (hereafter DMs) form a functional category of lexical items including both connecting devices signaling a discourse relation (e.g. *but, or, so*) and non-relational interactive discourse markers (e.g. *you know, well*). Both types of items can be described as metadiscursive instructions given to the hearer on how to interpret an utterance (Brinton, 2008; Hansen, 2006) or in other words as items encoding procedural meaning (Blakemore, 2002; Sperber and Wilson, 1993). Existing descriptions of DMs are often designed from the perspective of either the spoken or the written mode. There is however no principled reason for this separation, as many DMs like *so* or *because* are equally used in both modes, although in some cases with partially distinct functions. In order to develop a principled comparison between the use of DMs in the spoken and the written modes, we present in this paper a first attempt to use a single taxonomy to annotate DMs across both the spoken and written modes.

While DMs have a number of syntactic and prosodic features, the annotation scheme described in this paper targets their meanings only. We report more specifically two annotation experiments that were conducted in order to evaluate the replicability of a functional tag set (Crible, 2014), originally designed for spoken French and English, to written corpora on the same languages. In the first experiment, we tested the application of definitional criteria in order to select candidate tokens of DMs in corpus data. In the second experiment, we used a functional tag set to annotate the meaning of these DMs in four corpora encompassing two languages (English and French) in the spoken and the written modes.

The paper is structured as follows. In Section 2, we introduce a functional definition of DMs and briefly discuss the taxonomy of relations used in our experiments. In Section 3, we present the data and methodology used for the selection of DMs and discuss the results from this experiment. In Section 4, we report the sense annotation experiment and compare inter-annotator agreement across the two languages and modes tested. We conclude in Section 5 and present some perspectives for future work.

2 Defining a taxonomy of discourse markers applicable to spoken and written data

Studies attempting to provide definitions for the category of DMs are numerous, but no consensus has been reached yet on the list of features characterizing this category. Definitions vary greatly depending on the framework and the type of data that is included: monolingual vs. multilingual corpora, written vs. spoken mode, genres or situations (e.g. more or less formal). This rather chaotic situation is caused by the formal heterogeneity of these pragmatic items, which can only be grouped by their overarching function, *viz.* their role as metadiscursive interpretation cues encoding the speaker's internal representation of discourse in a hearer-oriented design. Authors usually agree on including conjunctions (*but, because, although*), some adverbs (*actually, well*), particles (*oh, hum*), prepositional phrases (*in fact, in other words*) and verbal phrases (*you know, I mean*), although within syntactic and pragmatic restrictions such as "weak-clause association" (Schourup, 1999) or non-referential meaning. For the present research, we used the following definition of DMs, based on Crible (2014):

> Syntactically optional, non-truth-conditional expressions constraining the inferential mechanisms of interpretation processes. They function on a metadiscursive level as a cue to situate the host unit in a co-built representation of on-going discourse. They do so by either signaling a discourse relation between the host unit and its context, marking the structural sequencing of discourse segments, expressing the speaker's meta-comment on their phrasing, or contributing to interpersonal collaboration.

This definition is functional, inclusive and can therefore capture the various ways in which different languages encode discourse structure as well as the complexity of spontaneous oral conversations, which are a privileged source of linguistic creativity. DMs are indeed more frequent and more varied (formally and functionally) in speech, where they also co-exist with other pragmatic phenomena such as disfluencies, politeness expressions, interjections, or modal particles with which they can be particularly confusing, as noted by Cuenca (2013) who talks of "fuzzy boundaries" between modal marking and discourse marking for example.

Crible (2014) designed an annotation protocol following the above definition of the category of DMs. To structure the multifunctionality of its members, four functional "domains" (Sweetser, 1990) have been identified from a critical review of previous works (Gonzalez, 2005, Halliday and Hasan, 1976; Redeker, 1990) and their empirical soudness when applied to corpus data. These domains correspond to macro-functions of DMs and each one includes a list of possible values, twenty-nine in total:

- Ideational: relations between real-world events. Includes cause, consequence, contrast, concession, condition, alternative, temporal, exception;
- Rhetorical: relations between epistemic and speech-act events, and metadiscursive functions. Includes motivation, conclusion, opposition, relevance, reformulation, approximation, comment, specification, emphasis;
- Sequential: structuration of discourse segments. Includes: opening boundary, closing boundary, topic-resuming, topic-shifting, quoting, enumerating, punctuating, addition;
- Interpersonal: interactive management of the speaker-hearer relationship. Includes: monitoring, face-saving, agreeing, disagreeing.

This taxonomy was designed to meet the balance between extensive coverage of all possible functions of DMs as they are usually described in the literature, i.e. from coherence relations ("because") to more interactional uses ("you know"), and on the other hand, intensive, precise definition of the different categories so that they do not overlap. A similar fourfold system can be found in Haselow (2011), although without any operational criteria. These domains are defined and motivated with more detail in the annotation protocol.

The multifunctionality of DMs is also reflected in the scheme by the possibility to assign simultaneously two tags, either from the same domain or from two different ones. This accounts for the polysemy of some DMs and their ability to encode several meanings (e.g. Petukhova and Bunt, 2009), as in the following examples of (1) cause and temporal relations (both ideational) and (2) opposition (rhetorical) and topic-shift (sequential):

(1) "Rising dismay at Honohan's judgment crystallised into outright scepticism **after** an extraordinary interview with Bloomberg business news on May 28th last year." (COMTIS corpus, 210).

(2) "I think I've learnt a lot more in the intervening years and it might be nice to go back and work on those. **But** essentially since then I've been working pretty much full-time on trying to write poetry" (Backbone bb_en025 "creative writing").

As opposed to the Penn Discourse Treebank (PDTB) (Prasad et al., 2007), this model differentiates a function in one domain from its equivalent in another, for instance ideational cause and its rhetorical counterpart, motivation. Distinction of these frequent pairs at the first level of annotation allows for each tag to be autonomous and direct, while the PDTB suggests a system of levels, starting from a generic term (e.g. "contingency") and then specifying in several sublevels the particular meaning (e.g. "cause"; "reason" or "result"; "pragmatic" or "non-pragmatic"). Apart from this difference, the present model generally adopts the general approach to DMs as proposed by the theory-neutral and lexically-based framework of the PDTB[1], and more specifically its revision by Zufferey and Degand (2014).

The PDTB taxonomy was designed for written data and has scarcely been applied to spoken corpora (Demirsahin and Zeyrek, 2014; Tonelli et al., 2010). Our tag set has been adapted to speech using a corpus-based methodology: the original taxonomy was tested on spoken corpora and modified in order to better account for the specificities of this mode as they were encountered in authentic data. Therefore, the innovation of the research described here is to assess to what extent the twenty-nine functions identified by Crible (2014) are, in return, applicable to the written mode. Our goal is to reach a single multimodal annotation scheme, in order to prevent the multiplicity of frameworks and their lack of communicability[2].

3 Experiment 1: identification of candidate DMs

3.1 Data and procedure

The first experiment consisted in the identification of occurrences of discourse markers by two expert coders, with French as mother tongue and excellent proficiency in English. Although both have experience in the multilingual annotation of discourse markers, one is a specialist in written corpora while the other works with spoken corpora.

The dataset used to test the identification of DMs was comprised of four texts of ca.1000 words each, in spoken and written French and English, from the spoken corpus of face-to-face interviews *Backbone* (Kurt, 2012) and the written corpus of newspaper articles collected by the COMTIS project[3].

We proceeded in two steps: first, identification in the written texts, based on the assumption that they would be less problematic to annotate; then in the spoken texts, once potential issues had been identified. The selection on written texts was performed without prior discussion of the category, but merely using its definition from the annotation scheme as stated above. After discussion of the disagreements and identification of recurring problems, we moved on to the selection of DMs in the spoken texts.

[1]As opposed to relation-based frameworks like Rhetorical Structure Theory (e.g. Taboada, 2006) or Segmented Discourse Representation Theory (Asher and Lascarides, 2003) which analyze and annotate discourse spans or relations, rather than the discourse markers themselves, thus involving heavier theoretical background.

[2]This work is conducted as part of the ongoing COST Action Network TextLink (IS1312) "Structuring Discourse in Multilingual Europe", chair: L. Degand. `http://textlinkcost.wix.com/textlink`.

[3]`http://www.idiap.ch/project/comtis`

3.2 Results and discussion

The results from the identification experiment are reported in Table 1.

	Coder 1	Coder 2	Selected by both	Relative agreement	Missing in coder 2	Added in coder 2
EN_sp	54	70	51	82.25%	3	19
FR_sp	81	77	69	87.34%	12	8
EN_wr	20	28	19	79.16%	1	**9**
FR_wr	19	26	15	66.67%	4	**11**

Table 1: Absolute and relative agreement on the independent selection of DMs

At a general level, it is noticeable that the annotation of DMs in written texts is not easier than in spoken corpora, even though spoken data is often more diverse and complex to annotate than planned speech. DMs in writing are thus not particularly easier to identify, as demonstrated by the high number of disagreements[4] in this mode as well. However, the types of disagreement are different in the two modes. For instance, in writing, some coders include temporal connectives and prepositional phrases such as *in order to*, which can be problematic if not specifically addressed in the annotation scheme. The relevant criterion that resolved this confusion was that of semantic-syntactic independence (i.e. completion, autonomy) of the connected unit, which, in the case of *in order to*, would not be met by the following infinitive clause. On the other hand, speech-specific phenomena like turn-initial response signals (*okay, yeah*) or fillers may confuse the selection, since they are sometimes considered as DMs in the literature given their pragmatic function. Here, the annotation scheme must specify the precise conditions under which such expressions can be selected as tokens of DMs.

Finally, we also found that coders have different biases depending on their area of expertise. More specifically, coders identify more potential candidates in the modality they are more used to work with: we can observe that coder 2 (expert in writing) identified more tokens in the written texts (cf. bold-faced cells in the table). This result advocates for enhanced training and discussions even between expert coders, and a more prescriptive definition of the DM category than was originally provided by the protocol. As a result, the final version of the definition lists the following criterial features for the selection of candidate tokens:

- procedural meaning within one of the four functional domains;
- syntactic optionality: their removal does not alter the grammaticality of the utterance;
- scope over syntactically and semantically independent units: there must be a finite or implicit predicate, which excludes relative and non-finite clauses, and nominal phrases except when these are acting as a-verbal predicates;
- high degree of grammaticalization: fixed multi-word units, frequently used (not idiosyncratic) and semantically non-compositional;
- incompatibility with membership in the categories of fillers, interjections, response signals, epistemic parentheticals, general extenders, tag questions and editing terms.

Although the authors have not yet tested the extent to which this new definition improves the identification process, the boundaries between DMs and similar expressions are more directly addressed than they were before. Motivations for theses choices are detailed in the annotation protocol.

[4]Kappa scores could not be computed given the unequal number of responses between coders. The percentages represent the ratio of commonly chosen DMs on the total number of tokens selected by both coders.

4 Experiment 2: annotation of discourse functions

4.1 Data and procedure

In both languages, the corpora used in this experiment contained ca.1500 words for speech and 3100 words for writing, in different texts from the same corpora as above (Kurt, 2012 and COMTIS project). In each subcorpus (written and spoken, French and English), we annotated 100 tokens of DMs. For the spoken texts, we didn't use sound files in order to keep the annotation process as comparable as possible in both modes, even though this has been showed in previous research to increase the level of inter-annotator agreement for the identification of DMs (Zufferey and Popescu-Belis, 2004). The functional annotation was performed on DMs selected by one coder only, in order to prevent selection-related disagreements in this experiment.

As in experiment 1, we started the annotation without prior discussion of the guidelines but only used the instructions as they were provided by the annotation protocol, as any isolated researcher would do in the same situation. This was done in order to evaluate the self-sufficiency of the protocol. The instructions were presented in the form of a list of function tags (e.g. cause), the definition for each tag (e.g. "causality of two real-world events"), criteria for the use and disambiguation of tags (e.g. "applies to facts, even future or hypothetical events"), sometimes a paraphrase for specifically ambiguous functions (e.g. "this happened because") and authentic examples from the *Backbone* spoken corpus (Kurt, 2012) (e.g. "they do struggle because sometimes it's their first experience").

We performed the annotation independently in the following order: written French, spoken French, written English, spoken English. Disagreements were discussed after the annotation of each sub-corpus, thus progressively improving the scheme by making each problematic bias or boundary more explicit when possible. Cases of double tags (i.e. when two simultaneous functions were assigned to the same item) were not counted as disagreements when at least one tag was common to both coders.

4.2 Results and discussion

The results from the sense annotation experiment are reported in Table 2[5].

Corpus	Percentage of agreement
written French	44%
spoken French	52%
written English	34%
spoken English	49%

Table 2: Inter-rater agreement scores on sense annotation

These results seem to indicate that spoken data may be easier to annotate than written data, as the level of inter-annotator agreement is always higher. However, as spoken corpora were annotated after written corpora in both languages, this result might also reflect the effect of training. The latter effect was not carried over between the two languages however, as annotations in English did not lead to a better agreement than in French, even though it was performed after discussions of the two French corpora. This may be due to the fact that the annotators are not native speakers of English, which may have caused more uncertainties about the senses conveyed by DMs. Indeed, previous research has shown that learners have uncertain judgments about the correct and incorrect uses of connectives when their L1 produces negative transfer effects, even at advanced stages of language learning (Zufferey et al., to appear).

For all corpora, the sources of disagreement were located in three dimensions. The first problem was the distinction between ideational and rhetorical relations. As mentioned above, the annotation scheme

[5] Again, the incremental process of the annotation did not allow us to compute kappa scores since the successive annotation rounds were not independent of each other. However, mere percentages have been used elsewhere in similar cases, for example in the PDTB (e.g. Miltsakaki et al., 2008).

encodes this difference in the functional tags themselves, and not as a separate level as in the PDTB. Despite the benefits of a direct use of tags exposed above (see section 2), many problems originated from these disambiguations, as in examples (3) and (4):

(3) "I've begun to take my writing a little bit more seriously in the sense that I see it as part of what I do professionally as well as personally, and **so** I've started trying to develop more of a profile" (*Backbone* en_025 "creative writing")

(4) "you've got rhythms, you've got cadence, you've got rhyme schemes potentially, you've got possibilities of evoking visual scenarios, possibilities of evoking sounds and **so** it's very multimodal" (*Backbone* en_025 "creative writing")

The token "so" in (3) signals a semantic (ideational) relation between the fact of "taking one's writing more seriously" and "trying to develop a profile", while in (4), the speaker introduces more of a conclusion, an epistemic (rhetorical) consequence between a number of features of poetry and its evaluation as being multimodal. These examples illustrate how complex it is to grasp the thin line between facts of personal history (3) and personal evaluation of facts (4), as authors/speakers are somehow always involved in their discourse, although not to the same extent.

The second issue concerned the distinctions between semantically overlapping functions, such as conclusion vs. reformulation, addition vs. specification, opening boundary vs. topic-shift, which have close meanings from the same domain. Ambiguity of these functions (and of their criteria as defined in the protocol) is thus responsible for a great number of disagreements.

The third source of disagreement was our discovery of missing functions in the taxonomy, such as a tag encoding the meaning of "goal", to annotate tokens of DMs like *in order to*. This particular issue was addressed by assimilating the missing function to an existing tag ("goal" was grouped with "consequence" as was recommended by the PDTB) so that no *ad hoc* category was needed. Moreover, if certain functions simply do not exist in writing because they require a two-way interaction, some features of writing related to DMs did seem to emerge from our experiment, namely rhetorical or emphatic addition (furthermore", French "en outre", "de plus") and start of a new paragraph. The former was assimilated to the existing value "addition" with a small modification in the definition of the function, while the latter was grouped with "opening boundary" which, in speech, corresponds to a new turn of speech. Again, we chose not to create ad hoc categories but to try and integrate written specificities into the existing tag set.

We also observed that the annotation of spoken and written data involved different kinds of mode-specific problems. For instance, a recurring problem in spoken texts was the use of tags for speech-specific functions (e.g. monitoring, punctuating), given the inherent ambiguity of their "bleached" meaning and their absence in written texts. These particular functions were complex to agree upon, since their core meaning is not as explicit as a more traditional DM such as *because*, or a more monosemous expression such as *for example* which almost always expresses specification. Punctuating DMs, on the other hand, can take various forms (*well, I mean, I don't know, then*, etc.) and are thus less consensually identified.

Another cross-modal issue is the perceived boundary between ideational and rhetorical relations: in writing, subjectivity and interactivity are much less tangible than in speech where speakers often express their direct opinion and involve the hearer in their speech. Such medium-related tendencies led to a different bias, again reflecting each coder's expertise: coder 2 (expert in writing) would include more tokens as "pragmatic" DMs as soon as the writer's opinion is involved (as in example (5)), when coder 1 would have a more restricted understanding of "pragmatic" which is consistent with the high subjectivity of speech and requires a stronger involvement of the speaker (as in (6)), here expressed as a clear judgement or interpretation, instead of a factual event.

(5) "Les nouveaux taux devraient être supportables en Allemagne, **mais** ils vont précipiter plus avant dans le gouffre le marché immobilier et les banques" (COMTIS, 209).
The new rates should be bearable in Germany, ***but*** *they will plunge further into the abyss the real estate marker and the banks.*

(6) "Si tout se passe comme prévu, ce qui est d'ailleurs toujours le cas, la dette publique irlandaise atteindra les 250 milliards d'euros, **mais** ces différences sont sans importance." (COMTIS, 210).
If everything goes as planned, which is by the way always the case, the Irish national debt will reach 250 billion euros, ***but*** *these differences do not matter.*

As a result of this annotation experiment, the present annotation scheme was improved by: a greater precision in the criteria used to disambiguate similar functions (e.g. contrast vs. concession, temporal ordering vs. consequence); the systematic addition of a paraphrase for each possible value; the inclusion of specific sections in the protocol dedicated to ambiguous meanings (frequent polysemous DMs such as *and, but, so* etc. and semantic-pragmatic pairs). But this further operationalization of the taxonomy is only a qualitative, yet valuable, assessment of the methodological improvements. What inter-rater agreement analysis brings to light, and the main point of this study, is primarily the realization that many decisions that we make as annotators are implicitly biased, which leads to inevitable disagreement if not documented in the annotation scheme. Another lesson from our experiment is the necessity of training, even for expert coders, and the importance of discussing problems and decisions before launching a large-scale annotation campaign.

5 Conclusion

In this paper, our aim was to report two annotation experiments designed to assess the applicability of a functional definition of the category of DMs in order to reliably identify them in corpus data, and to assess the use of a taxonomy for DMs originally designed for speech to both spoken and written data. The results demonstrate that annotating spoken data does not lead to lower agreements compared to written data, contrary to what was expected. In addition, the differences between spoken and written data are located in the types of disagreements that they generate. However, this primarily qualitative evaluation of the taxonomy would require more data and a more systematic annotation procedure to validate these tentative results.

More generally, this pilot study makes yet another case for training and discussion while conducting annotation by several coders, and stresses the importance of a well-documented annotation scheme which provides detailed instructions and potential transfers between its tag set and other frameworks or data types, as the level of inter-annotator agreement systematically increases from the first to the second annotation performed within a language. The fact that this improvement was not carried over between the two languages reflects the fact that the marking of discourse structure is variable, even between typologically related languages (e.g. Degand, 2004; Pit, 2007; Zufferey and Cartoni, 2012), and the meanings and usage of discourse markers are therefore always at least partially language-specific. Indeed, languages vary in their encoding of discourse relations. To make a case in point, Dutch uses two specific connectives to convey ideational and rhetorical causes while English uses only one connective ("because"). French uses two specific connectives as well but one of them ("car") is also restricted to the written mode, creating register differences with Dutch.

The major outcome of this study is therefore not the quantitative reliability of the taxonomy, but rather the illustration of some methodological best practices for sense annotation in general, to raise awareness to recurring problems in discourse marker studies in particular.

Future perspectives for the annotation of DMs are the application of the coding scheme described in this paper to the modality of gestures (Bolly and Crible, 2015), the comparison of annotations performed by naive vs. expert coders (Crible and Degand, 2015), the annotation of DMs in speech with and without the help of prosody (i.e. with the sound files); and the comparison of inter-annotator agreement scores obtained by native and non-native speakers (e.g. a French coder annotating English data). Another perspective would be a comparative study between this multimodal annotation scheme and the ISO standard for discourse relations (Bunt et al., 2012) to situate the present approach within interoperable endeavours.

References

Asher, N. and A. Lascarides (2003). *Logics of Conversation.* Cambridge : CUP.

Blakemore, D. (2002). *Relevance and linguistic meaning. The semantics and pragmatics of discourse markers.* Cambridge : CUP.

Bolly, C. and L. Crible (2015). From context to functions and back again: Disambiguating pragmatic uses of discourse markers. In *International Pragmatics Association (IPrA) Conference, July 26-31, Antwerp, Belgium.*

Brinton, L. (2008). *The comment clause in English : syntactic origins and pragmatic development.* Cambridge : CUP.

Bunt, H., R. Prasad, and A. Joshi (2012). First steps towards an iso standard for annotating discourse relations. In *Proceedings of the Joint ISA-7, SRSL-3, and I2MRT LREC 2012 Workshop on Semantic Annotation and the Integration and Interoperability of Multimodal Resources and Tools*, Istanbul, Turkey.

Crible, L. (2014). Selection and functional description of discourse markers in french and english: towards crosslinguistic and operational categories for contrastive annotation. In *International Workshop - Pragmatic Markers, Discourse Markers and Modal Particles: What do we know and where do we go from here? October 16-17, Como, Italia.*

Crible, L. and L. Degand (2015). Functions and syntax of discourse connectives across languages and genres: Towards a multilingual annotation scheme. In *International Pragmatics Association (IPrA) Conference, July 26-31, Antwerp, Belgium.*

Cuenca, M. J. (2013). The fuzzy boundaries between discourse marking and modal marking. In L. Degand, B. Cornillie, and P. Pietrandrea (Eds.), *Discourse markers and modal particles. Categorization and description*, pp. 191–216. Amsterdam : John Benjamins.

Degand, L. (2004). Contrastive analyses, translation, and speaker involvement: the case of *puisque* and *aangezien*. In M. Achard and S. Kemmer (Eds.), *Language, Culture and Mind*, pp. 1–20. Stanford: CSLI Publications.

Demirsahin, I. and D. Zeyrek (2014). Annotating discourse connectives in spoken turkish. In *LAW VIII - The 8th Linguistic Annotation Workshop*, pp. 105–109.

Gonzalez, M. (2005). Pragmatic markers and discourse coherence relations in english and catalan oral narrative. *Discourse studies 77(1)*(1), 53–86.

Halliday, M. A. K. and R. Hasan (1976). *Cohesion in English.* London : Longman.

Hansen, M.-B. M. (2006). A dynamic polysemy approach to the lexical semantics of discourse markers (with an exemplary analysis of french toujours). In K. Fischer (Ed.), *Approaches to discourse particles*, pp. 21–41. Amsterdam : Elsevier.

Haselow, A. (2011). Discourse marker and modal particle : the functions of utterance-final *then* in spoken english. *Journal of Pragmatics 43*(14), 3603–3623.

Kurt, K. (2012). Pedagogic corpora for content and language integrated learning. insights from the backbone project. *The Eurocall Review 20*(2), 3–22.

Miltsakaki, E., L. Lee, and A. Joshi (2008). Sense annotation in the penn discourse treebank. *Lecture Notes in Computer Science 4919*, 275–286.

Petukhova, V. and H. Bunt (2009). Towards a multidimensional semantics of discourse markers in spoken dialogue. In *Proceedings of the 8th International Conference on Computational Semantics*, pp. 157–168.

Pit, M. (2007). Cross-linguistic analyses of backward causal connectives in dutch, german and french. *Languages in Contrast 7*(1), 53–82.

Prasad, R., E. Miltsakaki, N. Dinesh, A. Lee, and A. Joshi (2007). The penn discourse treebank 2.0 annotation manual. Technical report, Institute for Research in Cognitive Science.

Redeker, G. (1990). Ideational and pragmatic markers of discourse structure. *Journal of Pragmatics 14*(3), 367–381.

Schourup, L. (1999). Discourse markers. *Lingua* (107), 227–265.

Sperber, D. and D. Wilson (1993). Linguistic form and relevance. *Lingua 90*, 1–25.

Sweetser, E. (1990). *From etymology to pragmatics*. Cambridge : CUP.

Taboada, M. (2006). Discourse markers as signals (or not) of rhetorical relations. *Journal of Pragmatics 38*, 567–592.

Tonelli, S., G. Riccardi, R. Prasad, and A. Joshi (2010, may). Annotation of discourse relations for coconversation spoken dialogs. In N. C. C. Chair), K. Choukri, B. Maegaard, J. Mariani, J. Odijk, S. Piperidis, M. Rosner, and D. Tapias (Eds.), *Proceedings of the Seventh International Conference on Language Resources and Evaluation (LREC'10)*, Valletta, Malta, pp. 2084–2090. European Language Resources Association (ELRA).

Zufferey, S. and B. Cartoni (2012). English and french causal connectives in contrast. *Languages in contrast 12*(2), 232–250.

Zufferey, S. and L. Degand (2014). Representing the meaning of discourse connectives for multilingual purposes. *Corpus Linguistics and Linguistic Theory 10*.

Zufferey, S., W. Mak, L. Degand, and T. Sanders (to appear). Advanced learners' comprehension of connectives. the role of l1 transfer across online and offline tasks.

Zufferey, S. and A. Popescu-Belis (2004). Towards automatic identification of discourse markers in dialogues: the case of *like*. In *5th SIGdial Workshop on Discourse and Dialogue, Cambridge (MA)*, pp. 63–71.

Creating and retrieving tense and aspect annotations with GraphAnno, a lightweight tool for multi-level annotation

Volker Gast
Friedrich Schiller University Jena
volker.gast@uni-jena.de

Lennart Bierkandt
Friedrich Schiller University Jena
post@lennartbierkandt.de

Christoph Rzymski
Friedrich Schiller University Jena
christoph.rzymski@uni-jena.de

1 Introduction

In this paper, we propose an annotation scheme for the manual annotation of tense and aspect in natural language corpora, as well as an implementation using GraphAnno, a configurable tool for manual multi-level annotation. The annotation scheme is based on Klein's (1994) theory of tense and aspect, arguably the most widely accepted theory in this domain (cf. also Klein and Li 2009). One of the most important features of Klein's theory is that in addition to the time span during which a situation obtains (the 'time of situation'/TSit), it makes use of the concept of 'Topic Time' (TT), which is related to, but different from, Reichenbach's (1947) reference point 'R' (cf. Derczynski and Gaizauskas 2013). Given that the resulting annotations cannot be mapped one-to-one to words or constituents, and as they are partially retrieved from the context, a semantic layer of annotation is needed, in addition to the structural one. The multi-level approach advocated here also allows us to annotate temporal relations across sentences.

Section 2 provides some background on GraphAnno. Some ontological prerequisites of the annotation of tense and aspect are established in Section 3, and the concept of 'Topic Time' is introduced. Sections 4 and 5 demonstrate the annotation of temporal relations within and beyond the sentence, respectively. Section 6 describes the query language of GraphAnno, and Section 7 contains an outlook.

2 Some background on GraphAnno

GraphAnno was originally designed as a prototype for a more powerful annotation tool, Atomic (cf. Druskat et al. 2014), in a project on multi-level annotation of cross-linguistic data.[1] The tool has been used in various corpus-based projects (e.g. Gast 2015), and it has proven a stable and user-friendly application. Moreover, GraphAnno has some functions that Atomic lacks, specifically for searching and filtering (cf. Sect. 6 and Gast et al. 2015). It was therefore published in 2014, and will continue to be maintained.[2]

GraphAnno is so called because the corpus data is program-internally represented, and also visually displayed, as a graph, consisting of annotated nodes and edges. The application is platform-independent, but it requires Graphviz[3] and Ruby.[4] It handles dependencies on other libraries using the RubyGems package manager. An exe-file for easy use on a Windows system is available, bundling the required Ruby runtime environment. The tool has a browser-based interface and is operated via a command line at the bottom of the browser window. Annotations are created with one-letter commands such as `n` (create a node), `g` (grouping nodes into constituents), `e` (create an edge), `d` (deleting nodes or edges) and `a` (annotation of nodes and edges with attribute-value pairs), followed by their arguments. Navigation

[1] LinkType, sponsored by the German Science Foundation (DFG, grant GA-1288/5). Financial support from this institution is gratefully acknowledges; see also http://www.linktype.iaa.uni-jena.de. [2] https://github.com/LBierkandt/graph-anno
[3] http://www.graphviz.org [4] http://www.ruby-lang.org

and additional functions such as filtering, searching and configurations are accessed and controlled with key bindings and function keys.

GraphAnno has an import function, and some preprocessing functionalities are implemented, e.g. punkt segmenters. It uses JSON-files for native storing. Scripts and converters are available or under construction for other corpora, e.g. the BioScope corpus (Vincze et al., 2008) and Timebank 1.2,[5] and for corpus formats like those accessible through NLTK[6] modules.

3 The elements of time and tense annotation

We adopt Klein's (1994: Ch.4) 'Basic Time Concept'. Points in time are identified with real numbers ($r \in \mathbb{R}$), time spans are intervals ($i = [r_i, r_2]$). Relations between intervals, e.g. of anteriority, can be established by relating the temporal atoms of a time span to each other, for instance:

(1) i_1 is ANT(ERIOR) to i_2 iff:
$\forall a \in i_1, \forall b \in i_2$: $a < b$

The analysis and annotation of time and tense requires establishing a system of types of intervals and relations between such intervals. The first formal system of tense logic was proposed by Reichenbach (1947). Reichenbach (1947) uses three points in time, 'S' (the moment of speech), 'E' (the event) and 'R' (a reference point). S and E are obviously indispensable components of any theory of tense and aspect and are, more or less directly, also part of prominent annotation schemes such as the (ISO-)TimeML language (Pustejovsky et al., 2005; Schilder et al., 2007). However, TimeML does not provide for a reference point. This is one of the reasons why "[i]n many ways, TimeML's tense system is less expressive than that of Reichenbach's" (Derczynski and Gaizauskas, 2013, 6).

As Derczynski and Gaizauskas (2013, 1) note, many efforts are currently being made to improve "reference point management" in computational linguistics. While we believe that this is a promising and in fact necessary development, we refer to a more recent formal approach to tense and aspect. Reichenbach's system is known to exhibit some weaknesses, as was already pointed by Comrie (1981), among others, who published a monograph with a theory of his own a few years later (Comrie 1985; cf. also Declerck 1986). The most comprehensive theory of tense in a Reichenbachian tradition so far has been proposed by Klein (1994), and we think it is fair to say that in theoretical linguistics, Klein (1994) is regarded as a standard in this domain. As we see no reason to refer to the older and, in many ways, fragmentary system of Reichenbach (1947), while a more comprehensive and 'cleaner' follow-up theory is available in the form of Klein (1994), we refer to the latter theory in our proposal.

3.1 Klein's (1994) Topic Time

Like Reichenbach (1947), Klein (1994) uses three prime elements in his theory, which he calls 'time of utterance'/TU ($\approx$ Reichenbach's 'S'), 'time of situation'/TSit ($\approx$ 'E'), and ' Topic Time'/TT. Klein's Topic Time is similar, but not identical, to Reichenbach's reference point R (e.g. insofar as it can be an interval). It is "the time span to which a speaker's claim is confined" (Klein, 1994, 6). Let us consider an example for illustration. In (2) speaker A asks a question about a specific point in time, 6am yesterday, which is established as a Topic Time. Speaker B provides information about this Topic Time.

(2) A: What was the weather like at 6pm yesterday?
B: It was raining.

Example (2) already shows why we need multi-level annotations to capture a Reichenbach/Klein-style tense semantics: There is no structural constituent corresponding to the Topic Time in B's answer.

One of the most important distinctions that can be made using Klein's Topic Time is the one between the Simple Past and the Present Perfect in English. According to Klein (1994), the Simple Past is used

[5] http://www.timeml.org/site/timebank/timebank.html [6] https://www.nltk.org/

when TT is located before TU/t_0 (TT < t_0). The Present Perfect, by contrast, is used when TT includes the moment of utterance (TT $\supseteq$ t_0). Consider the examples in (3).

(3) a. I have lived in New York.
    b. I lived in New York.

Both (3a) and (3b) say that there is a situation of the type 'living in New York' in which the speaker participated, and which is located before t_0. The difference concerns the time spans about which information is provided. (3a) provides information about t_0. It could be paraphrased as '*It is now the case that* I have lived in New York', and a likely implicature is that 'I (*now*) know (what it is like to live in) New York'. (3b) makes a statement about a time span in the past. A likely context for (3b) would be a question like 'What did you do in 1987'? Note that the semantic difference between the Present Perfect and the Simple Past is reflected in the fact that the Present Perfect is only compatible with temporal adverbials denoting time spans which contain t_0, while the Simple Past only allows time spans that precede t_0.

Being an important component of tense logic in general, the distinction between TT and TSit has a number of further advantages in the context of text annotation. Narratives are organized around TTs, as has also been noticed by Derczynski and Gaizauskas (2013, 4) for Reichenbach's R: "Observations during the course of this work suggest that the reference time from one sentence will roll over to the next sentence, until it is repositioned explicitly by a tensed verb or time". The location of the Topic Time depends on the tense used. In the case of the Simple Past, TTs are lined up sequentially. The Progressive aspect, by contrast, does not have any such effect of 'TT advancement'. Consider the examples in (4).

(4) a. At 3pm, John sat on the chair, looked at his watch and sang a song.
    b. At 3pm, John was sitting on the chair, looking at his watch and singing a song.

In (4a), the events happen sequentially, and the Topic Times form a chain. (As a consequence, the situations are also in temporal sequence, being related to the Topic Time through the [perfective] aspect in each case.) In (4b), there is only one Topic Time, 3pm, and all events described in the sentence 'surround' it. This type tense configuration – TT being fully included in TSit – is exactly what characterizes the progressive aspect, according to Klein (1994). What the examples in (4) show is that the Topic Time needs to be specified for each event, and that it cannot be recovered on purely structural grounds.

3.2 The grammatical categories of tense and aspect

According to Klein (1994), tense is a relation between TU/t_0 and TT. The type of predication expressed by the grammatical category of tense thus takes the form shown in (5). The category 'Past' is regarded as a (morphological) feature, interpreted as a one-place predicate.

(5) $[\![\text{PAST}]\!] = \lambda i\ [i \text{ ANT } t_0]$

ASPECT expresses a relation between the TT and TSit. In (2) above, speaker B expresses that the Topic Time (6am) is fully included in TSit (the situation of raining). The denotation of the aspectual category 'progressive' can thus be represented as shown in (6).

(6) $[\![\text{PROG}]\!] = \lambda i \lambda s[i \subset s]$

4 Annotating structure and function

We will assume that, in English, tense and aspect are structurally represented in the form of features or, more precisely, attribute-value pairs. The VP *was sleeping* can be represented as shown in Figure 1.

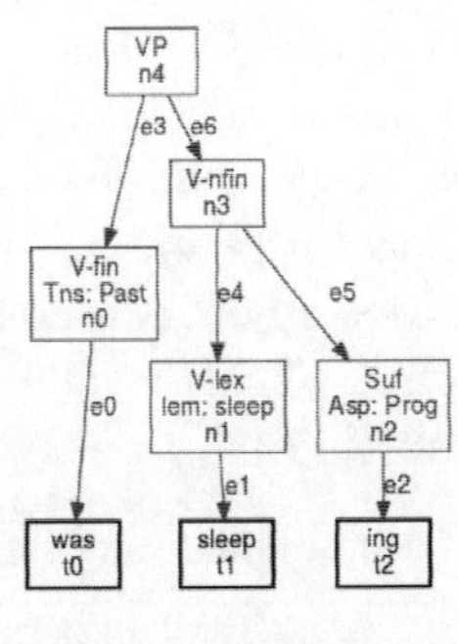

Figure 1: Structure

GraphAnno offers users the possibility to define a theoretically infinite number of levels of annotation, but we can work with the two levels that are preconfigured, a structural one (s-layer) and a functional one (f-layer). The tree in Figure 1 belongs to the structural layer. Annotations relating to tense and aspect can now be added on the f-layer. Denotations of nodes will be indicated according to the following conventions:

- Relations between intervals are indicated by capitalized abbreviations like 'ANT' (for anteriority).
- Predicates are separated from their arguments by a dash, the arguments are separated by a comma, e.g. 'IN-i,s' for 'i is included in s'.
- λ-bound variables are written between brackets, e.g. '[i]' for a λ-bound variable $\lambda i[\ldots i \ldots]$. The unsaturated predicate $\lambda i \lambda s[\text{ANT}(i)(s)]$ is thus represented as 'ANT-[i],[s]'.

In Figure 2, the s-layer is blue, the f-layer green. The nodes for the finite verb, the lexical verb and the progressive aspect marker are each linked to a node on the f-layer (Tns, Sit, Asp). The edges linking the functional nodes to the structural ones are of category 'dn', standing for 'denotation'. The [Past]-feature of the finite verb is interpreted as 'dn:[i]<t0'. The lexical predicate *sleep* denotes a situation (Sit) of sleeping. The [Prog]-feature (corresponding to the *ing*-suffix) denotes the progressive aspect, which, in accordance with Klein (1994), indicates that the Topic Time, TT, is fully included in the time of the situation, TSit. This is here represented as 'IN-[i],[s]' in the Asp-node.

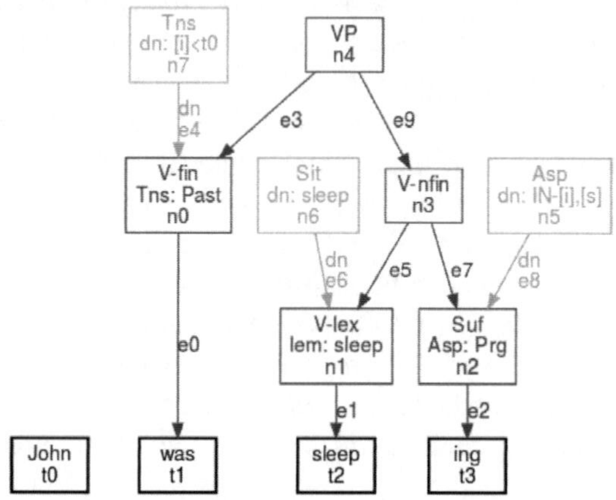

Figure 2: Nodes and their denotations

The temporal and aspectual predications can now be linked to their arguments. Every finite predicate is associated with a Topic Time. The (exact) Topic Time is mostly implicit (cf. below), but it can be made explicit with a temporal adverbial like *at six*. This adverbial denotes a (minimal) time span i, a point in time. We represent points in time in the format 'day/hour/minute/second'. A plus or minus sign indicates time specification relative to t_0. Accordingly, '-1/6/30/0' stands for 'one day before t_0 at 6:30 am'. Time nodes carry an s-attribut for the start and an e-attribute for the end of a time span. In the case of a point in time, the s- and e-attributes are identical. Figure 3 shows the graph in which the tense and aspect predications are linked to their arguments (some structural annotations are omitted for better visibility).[7] The relevant edges are labelled 'arg1' and 'arg2'.

Let us consider more complex cases like the ones in (7) (suggested to us by a reviewer):

(7) a. John taught three hours every week last semester.

b. John has been teaching at Oxford since 2009.

The Topic Time of (7a) is specified as 'every week last semester'. It can be interpreted as a generalized quantifier. As TT takes wide scope, it can be represented as shown in (8). The choice of tense (Simple Past) is in accordance with the fact that TT is located before t_0, and the perfective/non-progressive aspect is used because each instance of teaching (TSit) is fully included in each instance of w (TT).

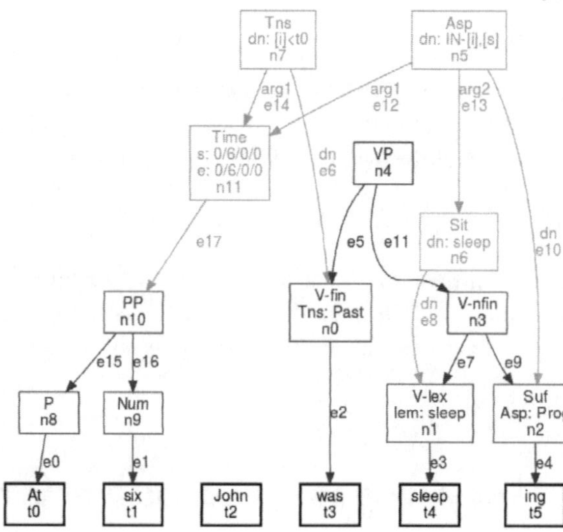

Figure 3: Nodes and relations between them

(8) $\forall w \subseteq [\![\text{last semester}]\!]$: John taught three hours in w

[7] Note that GraphAnno allows users to filter and hide elements with specific properties (such as membership to a given level) for better visibility; cf. Gast et al. (2015) for more information and illustration.

(7b) represents a well-known problem of English temporal semantics, the Present Perfect Progressive. We assume that this tense is interpreted in an additive manner, combining the meaning of the Perfect aspect (anteriority) with that of the Progressive aspect (inclusion of TT in TSit). It says that a sub-event of s, s', which is of the same type as s (teaching [someone]), is located before TT, and that TT is fully included in TSit. (7b) is thus interpreted as shown in (9). For the annotation graph, this means that two Asp-nodes will be linked to the same (Topic) Time node.

(9) for TT $= t_0$:

$$\exists y \exists s \exists s'_{\subseteq s} :$$

$$s = [2009, t_0] \wedge \text{TEACH}(y)(John)(s) \wedge \text{TEACH}(y)(John)(s') \wedge \underbrace{\text{TT} \subseteq s}_{\text{progressive}} \quad \wedge \underbrace{s' \leq \text{TT}}_{\text{perfect}}$$

5 Beyond the sentence

We now have a framework for the annotation of tense and aspect within the sentence. We want to be able to annnotate (and retrieve) temporal relations across sentences as well. In order to be able to annotate contextual, often implicit temporal information, we add 'context tokens', represented by a hash, at the beginning of each sentence. They contain information about the Topic Time. Implicit Topic Times are often identical to the preceding sentence, or they correspond to an immediately following time span.

Figure 4 shows an example (*He came at six. The sun had sunk*). Again, some structural annotations are omitted. The context node, here tokenized as `t5`, carries an annotation at the functional level which provides the Topic Time for the second sentence. It is copied from the first sentence. In this way text-level temporal structures can be annotated and, as we will see in the next section, retrieved.

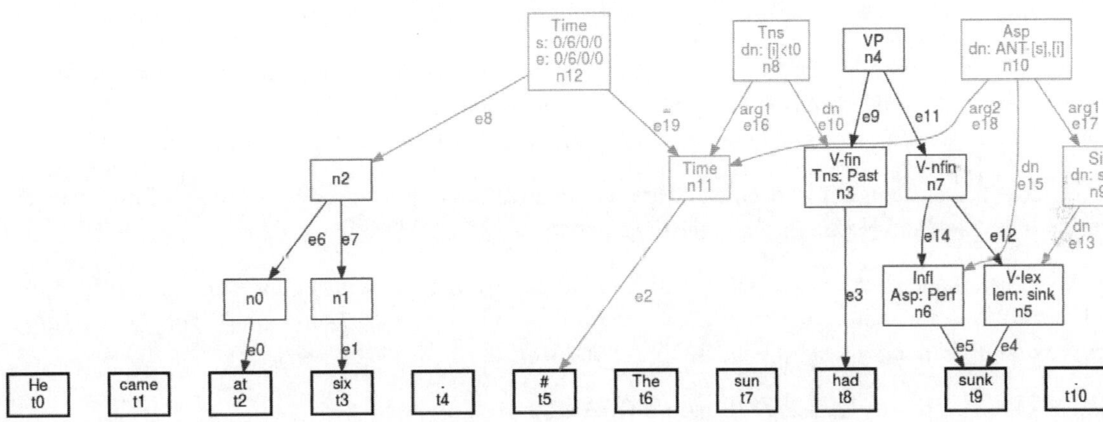

Figure 4: Annotations beyond the sentence boundary

6 Retrieving temporal configurations

GraphAnno also has a powerful yet transparent query language. The user specifies a graph fragment by describing it in terms of attribute-value pairs associated with nodes, as well as edges between nodes. The following query retrieves temporal configurations of the type shown in Figure 4.

(10)
```
node @a cat:Tns & dn:[i]<0          # define Past tense node
node @b cat:Asp & dn:ANT-[s],[i]    # define Perfect aspect node
node @c cat:Time                    # define Time node
edge @a@c                           # edge between @a and @c
edge @b@c                           # edge betweeb @a and @b
```

Any graph fragment matching the query is highlighted visually and can be exported into a data frame.

7 Outlook

We have focused on the manual annotation of tense and aspect configurations in English. The annotation scheme can be regarded as an implementation of Klein's (1994) theory of tense and aspect and is thus, as we believe, fully interpretable linguistically speaking. We hope to have shown that GraphAnno's unrestrictive approach to annotation allows for the implementation and subsequent testing of linguistic theories, without being specifically tailored to any specific theory.

Some of the semantic annotations used for illustration are obviously redundant (since predictable from structural ones) and can largely be automated. For instance, the denotations of morphological features like [Past] and [Prog] are largely (though not entirely) invariant. A more challenging task consists in figuring out the relationships between Topic Times across sentences. Annotation experiments will show to what extent such text-level annotations are amenable to meachine learning.

References

Comrie, B. (1981). On Reichenbach's approach to tense. In R. A. Hendrick, C. S. Masek, and M. F. Miller (Eds.), *Proceedings of the 7th meeting of the Chicago Linguistics Society*, pp. 24–30.

Comrie, B. (1985). *Tense*. Cambridge: Cambridge University Press.

Declerck, R. (1986). From Reichenbach (1947) to Comrie (1985) and beyond: Towards a theory of tense. *Lingua 70*, 305–364.

Derczynski, L. and R. Gaizauskas (2013). Empirical validation of Reichenbach's tense framework. In *Proceedings of the 10th International Conference on Computational Semantics*.

Druskat, S., L. Bierkandt, V. Gast, C. Rzymski, and F. Zipser (2014). Atomic: An open-source software platform for multi-level corpus annotation. In J. Ruppert and G. Faaß (Eds.), *Proceedings of the 12th Konferenz zur Verarbeitung natrlicher Sprache (KONVENS 2014), October 2014*, pp. 228–234.

Gast, V. (2015). On the use of translation corpora in contrastive linguistics: A case study of impersonalization in english and german. *Languages in Contrast 15*(1), 4–33.

Gast, V., L. Bierkandt, and C. Rzymski (2015). Annotating modals with GraphAnno, a configurable lightweight tool for multi-level annotation. In *Proceedings of the Workshop on Models for Modality Annotation, held in conjunction with IWCS 11, 2015*.

Klein, W. (1994). *Time in Language*. London: Routledge.

Klein, W. and P. Li (Eds.) (2009). *The Expression of Time*. Berlin: de Gruyter Mouton.

Pustejovsky, J., R. Ingria, R. Saurí, J. Castaño, J. Littman, R. Gaizauskas, and A. Setzer (2005). The specification language TimeML. In I. Mani, J. Pustejovsky, and R. Gaizauskas (Eds.), *The Language of Time: A Reader*. Oxford: Oxford University Press.

Reichenbach, H. (1947). *Elements of Symbolic Logic*. New York: Macmillan & Co.

Schilder, F., G. Katz, and J. Pustejovsky (Eds.) (2007). *Annotating, Extracting and Reasoning about Time and Events*. Heidelberg: Springer.

Vincze, V., G. Szarvas, R. Farkas, G. Móra, and J. Csirik (2008). The BioScope corpus: Biomedical texts annotated for uncertainty, negation and their scopes. *BMC Bioinformatics 9*(S-11).

The Semantics of Image Annotation

Julia Bosque-Gil
Universidad Politécnica de Madrid
Brandeis University
jbosque@delicias.dia.fi.upm.es

James Pustejovsky
Computer Science Department
Brandeis University
jamesp@cs.brandeis.edu

Abstract

This paper presents a language for the semantic annotation of images, focusing on event types, their participants, and their spatial and orientational configurations. This language, ImageML, is a self-contained *layered specification* language, building on top of ISOspace, as well as some elements from Spatial Role Labeling and SpatialML. An annotation language characterizing such features surrounding an event and its various aspects could play a significant role in structured image retrieval, and a mapping of annotated semantic entities and the image's low-level features will likely assist event recognition and description generation tasks.

1 Introduction

The role of image annotation is becoming increasingly important in the context of algorithms that allow for efficient access and retrieval of images from large datasets; for this reason, it has become an active topic of research in both the computer vision and natural language processing communities. Keyword annotation (tagging) approaches include interactive annotation games (Von Ahn and Dabbish, 2004; Von Ahn et al., 2006; Ho et al., 2009) and automatic keyword annotation, where, given an image, the system provides the appropiate (or potential) labels that describe its content (Li and Fei-Fei, 2007; Luo et al., 2009; Feng and Lapata, 2010). On the other hand, efforts in the task of image caption generation have experienced a growth due to the advances in object recognition. Here, objects as well as relations among them have to be identified, and the output must be a grammatical (and, if possible, natural) sentence that correctly describes the image content (Kiros et al., 2014). Approaches include those of Farhadi et al. (2010); Elliott and Keller (2013); Kiros et al. (2014) and Karpathy and Fei-Fei (2014), among many others.

The current MPEG-7 format encodes several dimensions of information about image structure (visual features, spatio-temporal structure, decomposition in regions or shots, etc.) and semantic content by means of its descriptors (Martinez, 2004). Semantic annotation with MPEG-7 captures events represented in the image as well as participants (objects and agents), the time, location, etc., and annotation and retrieval tools based on this format were presented in Lux et al. (2003); Lux and Granitzer (2005) and Lux (2009). The use of ontologies and thesaurus in the annotation of the semantic content of an image has been developed in the art history domain in Hollink et al. (2003); Hollink (2006) and Klavans et al. (2008), as well as in the context of multimedia semantic indexing (Nemrava et al. (2008)).

This paper approaches the annotation of image content outside the task of automatic image caption generation. Even though MPEG-7 approaches capture information about the event, its participants and the relations among them, this annotation could be enriched to include aspects that go beyond the basic categories addressed so far (location, time, event, participants), such as: the spatial relations between participants, the motion of objects, the semantic role of participants, their orientation and frame of reference, the relations among events in the image, or the characterization of the image as a whole as prototypical, given the event in question. These aspects can be included following text annotation schemes such as SpatialML (Mani et al., 2010), ISOspace (Pustejovsky et al., 2011) and Spatial Role Labeling (Kordjamshidi et al., 2010). Pustejovsky and Yocum (2014) in fact adapt ISOspace to the annotation of the spatial configuration of objects in image captions, in particular to distinguish the way captions refer to the structure versus the content of the image. In this paper, we introduce ImageML for this purpose, and we describe how this richer information concerning the image can be incorporated as a self-contained *layered annotation*[1], making explicit reference to several embedded specifications, i.e., ISO-TimeML and ISOspace (ISO/TC 37/SC 4/WG 2 (2014); Pustejovsky et al. (2010)).[2]

2 Problems Posed by Images

Text-based image search assumes that images have an annotation of some kind or at least a text in which to perform the query, and, that the text of the web page on which the image appears is related to the image content. These two assumptions, however, do not always hold. Content-based image retrieval approaches the problem by recording the image's low-level features (texture, color layout, etc.) and semantic annotation of images aims to bridge the gap between those low-level features and the image semantic content.

However, efforts in keyword annotation, MPEG-7-based semantic annotation, and ontology-based annotation do not capture some aspects to which users might turn their attention when searching for an image. Although unstructured labels might be enough for image filtering or simple queries (*dog running in park*), more complex ones require a richer annotation that includes a description about the orientation of figures with respect to the viewer, the spatial relations among objects, their motion, appearance, or the structure of the event (including it sub-events) in which they might be involved; e.g., a user needs a picture of someone running towards the camera while listening to music.

MPEG-7-based annotation effectively captures the 'narrative world' of the image (Benitez et al., 2002), but does not provide a thorough annotation of the representation of figures or a characterization of their motion according to different frames of reference. Furthermore, image captions alone have a fixed frame of reference (viewer) and descriptions might refer both to image structure or image content; cf. (Pustejovsky and Yocum, 2014), which makes the annotation of this distinction an important task towards a more accurate image retrieval.

By capturing information about: (1) the event (type of event, any sub-events, any motion triggered by it, or any other event the image might refer to, if it is ambiguous); (2) the participants of the event (their type of entity, their semantic roles, their appearance, and their representation); and (3) the setting and the time of the depicted situation, ImageML would not only contribute to a more precise image querying capability, but it could also assist in event recognition and automatic caption generation tasks.

3 Annotating Spatial Relations in Images with ISOspace

The annotation of spatial information in text involves at least the following: a PLACE tag (for locations, entities participating in spatial relations, and paths); LINK tags (for topological relations, direction and orientation, time and space measurements, and frames of reference); and a SIGNAL tag (for spatial prepositions)[3]. ISOspace has been designed to capture both spatial and spatiotemporal information as expressed in natural language texts (Pustejovsky et al. (2012)). We have followed a strict methodology of specification development, as adopted by ISO TC37/SC4 and outlined in Bunt (2010) and Ide and Romary (2004), and as implemented with the development of ISO-TimeML Pustejovsky et al. (2005) and others in the family of SemAF standards.

There are four spatial relation tags in ISOspace, that are relevant to the definition of ImageML, defined as follows:

(1) a. QSLINK – qualitative spatial relations;
    b. OLINK – orientation relations;
    c. MLINK – dimensions of a region or the distance between them.

[1]Roser and Pustejovsky (2008); Lee (2013).

[2]The initial specification of a semantic annotation for images is first outlined in Bosque-Gil (2014).

[3]For more information, cf. Pustejovsky et al. (2012).

d. MOVELINK – for movement relations;

QSLINKs are used in ISOspace to capture topological relationships between tag elements captured in the annotation. The `relType` attribute values come from an extension to the RCC8 set of relations that was first used by SpatialML. The possible RCC8+ values include the RCC8 values Randell et al. (1992), in addition to IN, a disjunction of TPP and NTPP.

Orientation links describe non-topological relationships. A SPATIAL_SIGNAL with a DIRECTIONAL `semantic_type` triggers such a link. In contrast to qualitative spatial relations, OLINK relations are built around a specific frame of reference type and a reference point. The `referencePt` value depends on the `frame_type` of the link. The ABSOLUTE frame type stipulates that the `referencePt` is a cardinal direction. For INTRINSIC OLINKs, the `referencePt` is the same identifier that is given in the `ground` attribute. For RELATIVE OLINKs, the identifier for the viewer should be provided as to the `referencePt`. When the document type is IMAGE, all `olinks` are interpreted as relative FR relations (unless otherwise stated), with the "VIEWER" as the `referencePt`.

ISOspace also allows one to identify the source and type of the text being annotated. This is done with the `document creation location` (DCL) attribute. This is a distinguished location that serves as the "narrative or reference location". While useful for narratives and news articles, captions associated with images pose a different problem, in that the document describes a *representational artifact*,[4] such as an image or a Google *Street View* scene; hence, the document type is distinguished as an IMAGE. To account for this, (Pustejovsky and Yocum, 2014) introduce a new attribute, `domain`, which can take one of two values: STRUCTURE and CONTENT. This allows the spatial relations to differentiate the kinds of regions being identified in the caption. Furthermore, this means that the DCL can take two values: an *Image Structure Location*, for reference to the image as an object; and an *Image Content Location*, which is what the picture refers to (as in the default DCL for most texts).

4 The ImageML Model

In this section, we describe ImageML, a model for the semantic annotation of images. The conceptual schema provides a introduction to the information covered, its elements, and the relations among them.

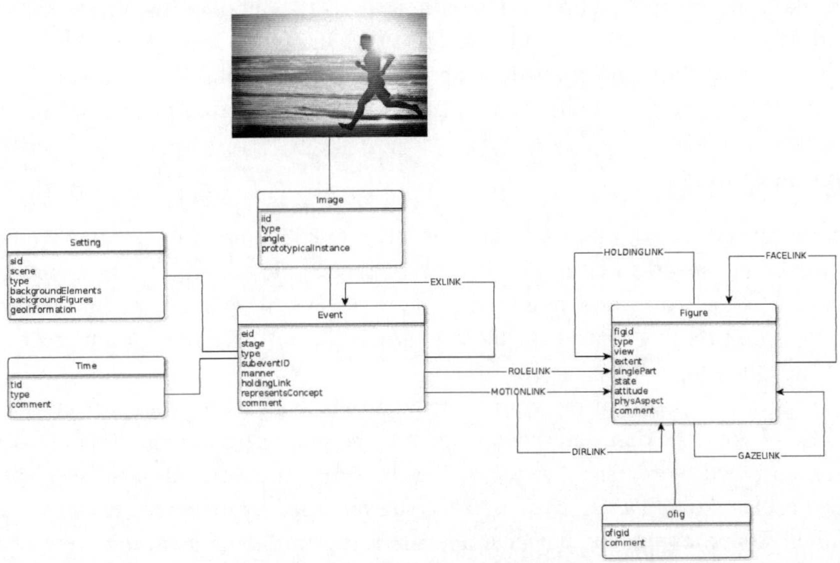

Figure 1: Conceptual Schema

[4]These are represented as $phys\_obj \bullet info$ complex types (dot objects), and inherit the properties of both type elements Pustejovsky (1995).

This annotation model is an attempt at capturing the semantic of images representing events, in contrast to images of landscapes and other non-dynamic representations. For this reason every annotated image includes at least one element of type EVENT.

The tags EVENT, FIGURE, OFIGURE, SETTING and TIME aim at encoding most of the information about the represented situation, both from a semantic perspective as well as from a formal one dealing with the specific way the elements are portrayed. In our view, participants of events have certain characteristics, such as their physical appearance or their type (an object, a person, etc.), are involved in events that affect their posture (eg. sitting, standing), might have a gesture that viewers interpret as them having an emotional attitude (which is valuable information for image descriptions), and are represented in a limited number of ways with respect to the viewer (back view, full body, etc.). Relation tags serve three purposes: first, capturing how a figure relates to an event and how the figure's specific representation is coupled with the characteristics of the motion involved in the event (if any); second, accounting for event ambiguity; and third, recording frequent sub-events of a main event which involve two participants (eg. holding, gazing, facing). We included the latter relations because they provide information that complements topological and spatial annotations without overcomplicating the annotation task. The modeling of these latter events as relations responds to the need to capture them in numerous images.

4.1 IMAGE

This tag records the type of image (e.g. photo) and the camera angle. Going back to Bloehdorn et al. (2005)'s knowledge base of prototypical instances, its attribute `prototypical` encodes whether an image could be considered a canonical instance of the event it depicts, which is valuable information for the event recognition task.

4.2 EVENT

The EVENT tag comes from TimeML (Pustejovsky et al., 2003; ISO/TC 37/SC 4/WG 2, 2012) and here it captures the activity, event, or change of state that is represented in the image. Its attribute `stage` encodes the phase of the event and the attribute `type` indicates whether the event is a sub-event of a main event or the main event itself, in which case its sub-events are also listed as values for the attribute `subevents`. Holding events that on first sight could have been thought of as EVENTs of type *sub-event* are here captured by links (HOLDINGLINK) to facilitate the annotation process. In this way, in a picture of someone taking notes holding a notebook and a pencil, only the event *take notes* would be recorded as EVENT, in this case of type *main* and with two HOLDINGLINKs, one for the pen and one for the notebook.

4.3 FIGURE and OFIGURE

FIGUREs are those objects in an image that are participants of an event or are involved in a holding relation. An object takes part in an event if it plays a semantic role (agent, theme, experiencer, etc.) in it, which is captured by the ROLELINK relation. This point is worth mentioning in order to distinguish FIGUREs from other objects that appear on the image but do not take part in any event, hence their description is outside the scope of this specification.

The type of object is encoded in the `type` attribute, which takes its values from the ACE Entity types[5], from MPEG-7 semantic descriptor values (*object* and *person*), and from SpatialML (*place*). The way the figure is portrayed with respect to the viewer in terms of a vertical axis (*front*, *profile-lateral*, etc.) and its perceivable extent (*whole*, *waist_up*, etc.) are recorded by the attributes `view` and `extent` respectively. Other properties such as physical appearance, attitude, or their state (e.g., open, broken, etc.) are also accounted for.

Figures not present in the picture but inferred by the reader when interpreting the image content are captured by the OFIGURE tag. Common examples are images in which a figure interacts with the

[5]ACE: Automatic Content Extraction 2008 Evaluation Plan (ACE08), `http://www.itl.nist.gov/iad/mig//tests/ace/2008/doc/`.

viewer (waving the hand at the camera, for instance), or close-up shots where the agent is not visible. An example of this is given below in Figure (2).

Figure 2: The OFIG is the agent of the event stir, the spoon is just the instrument.

4.4 SETTING and TIME

The SETTING tag aims at capturing information about the location of the events, any background elements or any background figures taking part in an event. Its attribute `figureID` distinguishes the overall setting of the events (e.g. a street) from specific objects in the image in which the event takes place (reading on *a bench* on the street), which are FIGURES with a role. The `scene` attribute records general aspects about the background of the image (e.g., *outdoors* and the attribute `type` encodes more specific information (e.g., *street*). Similarly, the TIME tag, inspired by TimeML TIMEX tag, encodes the time of the events and information deducible from the background.

4.5 ROLELINK and HOLDINGLINK

Kordjamshidi et al. (2010) introduce an annotation scheme similar in design to the task of semantic role labeling and classifies the arguments of spatial expressions in terms of their spatial roles. In this spirit, the tag ROLELINK addresses some spatial relations by indicating the source or goal of a movement, but it manly encodes the semantic roles participants of events play, turning to the semantic roles used in VerbNet (Schuler, 2005): *agent, recipient, instrument, experiencer*, etc. The HOLDINGLINK relation was introduced in section 4.2 and stands for holding sub-events: it links a figure (agent) that holds a figure (theme). Just as events, these relations have a `manner` attribute.

Figure 3: HOLDINGLINK expresses a sub-event hold, in which one figure holds another figure.

4.6 MOTIONLINK and DIRLINK

The tag MOTIONLINK is taken directly from ISOspace's MOVELINK tag. It associates to the event that triggers the motion, general information about the causer of the motion, the source and goal of it, and the path and medium through which the motion occurs. The orientation of the motion according to the different frames of reference is captured by the DIRLINK (direction link) relation, which combines attributes from SpatialML RLINKs and ISOspace OLINKs. The idea is to record fine-grained information about the orientation of the movement from the perspective of the object in motion, the causer of the movement and the viewer.

Figure 4: The relations MOTIONLINK and DIRLINK encode motion and direction of the event.

4.7 FACELINK AND GAZELINK

The relations FACELINK and GAZELINK draw upon the idea that eye gaze is an important semantic cue for understanding an image (Zitnick and Parikh, 2013). Facing and gazing could be thought of sub-events, but are here captured as links in a way resembling the relation HOLDINGLINK introduced earlier. Further, since a figure facing another figure does not imply that it is actually directing its gaze towards it, the FACELINK tag accounts for the way two figures are oriented towards one another, whereas the GAZINGLINK tag encodes eye-gaze relations between the two figures.

Figure 5: FACELINK captures facing relations between figures. A figure facing another may not be looking at it. For this reason, eye-gaze is encoded with GAZELINK.

4.8 EXLINK

EXLINKs take as arguments at least two events and express the fact that they are mutually exclusive. Some images might be ambiguous in the event they represent: a plane landing or taking off, someone parking the car or maneuvering to leave the spot, closing or opening a book, etc. The idea behind including both potential events is to allow for an association of the same low level features to both types of events in the context of automatic event recognition as well as for a retrieval of the image if the user searches for images of any of the two events.

5 Annotation Examples

To illustrate the descriptive nature of ImageML, let us consider an image that exploits many of the specification elements described above. This image is an instance of someone taking notes in a notebook.[6] The associated annotation identifies the event as "note-taking", along with the attributes of "holding a pen", the setting as being an interior location, the background being a bookshelf, and so on.

[6]Extracted from Google Image Search. Source: Flicker user Marco Arment (*marcoarment*).

Figure 6: Brainstorming.

```
<IMAGE id="i0"  type="PHOTO" angle="NEUTRAL" prototypicalInstance="yes"/>
<FIGURE id="fig0"  type="PERSON" view="FRONT" extent="SINGLE_PART"
   singlePart="right hand and arm " state="" attitude="" physAspect="in a
   green sweatshirt" comment="">a student</FIGURE>
<FIGURE id="fig1"  type="OBJECT" view="PROFILE_LATERAL" extent="WHOLE"
   singlePart="" state="" attitude="" physAspect="black and silver"
   comment="">a pen</FIGURE>
<FIGURE id="fig2"  type="OBJECT" view="3/4" extent="INSIDE" singlePart=""
   state="open" attitude="" physAspect="spiral, square ruled" comment="">a
   college notebook</FIGURE>
<EVENT id="e0"  stage="DURING" type="MAIN_EVENT" subevent="e1" manner=""
   holdingLink="hl0" representsConcept="" comment="">take notes </EVENT>
<EVENT id="e1"  stage="DURING" type="SUB-EVENT" subevent="" manner=""
   holdingLink="" representsConcept="" comment=""> sit</EVENT>
<HOLDINGLINK id="hl0"  holderFigureID="fig0" heldFigureID="fig1"
   manner="in his right hand"/>
<ROLELINK id="rl0" figureID="fig0" eventID="e1" role="AGENT"/>
<ROLELINK id="rl1" figureID="fig1" eventID="e1" role="INSTRUMENT"/>
<ROLELINK id="rl2" figureID="fig2" eventID="e1" role="PLACE"/>
<SETTING id="l0"  figureID="" scene="INDOORS" type="FACILITY"
   backgroundElements="bookshelves" backgroundFigures=""
   geoInformation="">studying room</SETTING>
<TIME id="t0"  type="OTHER"></TIME>
```

Rather than merely annotating all events in the image equally, it is important to note that there is a topic event ("note-taking"), and that other salient eventualities, such the pen being held in a hand, etc., are captured as relational attributes to the main event. This would not be sufficient for a general event description protocol, such as that promoted in ISO-TimeML, but for image descriptions, it appears particularly well-suited, at least in the context of images that we have so far studied. Obviously, this is an issue that deserves further empirical study.

6 Conclusion

In this paper we have presented ImageML, a model for the semantic annotation of images which draws largely upon ISOspace, as well as some aspects of Spatial Role Labeling and SpatialML, to capture fine-grained information about the events depicted in an image, the motion involved (described from different frames of reference), as well as information about the participants, their orientation, and the relations among them. The setting and time of the situation are also accounted for. By its very design, ImageML is a layered annotation, incorporating elements and values from the embedded specification languages of ISOspace and ISO-TimeML.[7]

While not yet created, a database of images annotated with this information along with the spatial configuration of objects should be of potential use to structured image retrieval, event detection and recognition, and automatic image caption generation. We are currently pursuing the creation of such a corpus.

Acknowledgements

Julia Bosque-Gil was partially supported by the LIDER project: "Linked Data as an enabler of cross-media and multilingual content analytics for enterprises across Europe", a FP7 project reference number 610782 in the topic ICT-2013.4.1: Content analytics and language technologies. James Pustejovsky was partially supported by grants from NSF's IIS-1017765 and NGA's NURI HM1582-08-1-0018. All errors and mistakes are, of course, the responsibilities of the authors.

References

Benitez, Ana B, Hawley Rising, Corinne Jorgensen, Riccardo Leonardi, Alessandro Bugatti, Koiti Hasida, Rajiv Mehrotra, A Murat Tekalp, Ahmet Ekin, and Toby Walker (2002). Semantics of multimedia in mpeg-7. In *Proceedings of the International Conference on Image Processing*, Volume 1, pp. I–137. IEEE.

Bloehdorn, Stephan, Kosmas Petridis, Carsten Saathoff, Nikos Simou, Vassilis Tzouvaras, Yannis Avrithis, Siegfried Handschuh, Yiannis Kompatsiaris, Steffen Staab, and Michael G Strintzis (2005). Semantic annotation of images and videos for multimedia analysis. In *The semantic web: research and applications*, pp. 592–607. Springer.

Bosque-Gil, Julia (2014). *A Model for the Semantic Annotation of Images.* MA Thesis, Brandeis University.

Bunt, H. (2010). A methodology for designing semantic annotation languages exploiting syntactic-semantic iso-morphisms. In *Proceedings of ICGL 2010, Second International Conference on Global Interoperability for Language Resources.*

Elliott, Desmond and Frank Keller (2013). Image Description using Visual Dependency Representations. In *EMNLP*, pp. 1292–1302.

Farhadi, Ali, Mohsen Hejrati, Mohammad Amin Sadeghi, Peter Young, Cyrus Rashtchian, Julia Hockenmaier, and David Forsyth (2010). Every picture tells a story: Generating sentences from images. In *Computer Vision–ECCV 2010*, pp. 15–29. Springer.

Feng, Yansong and Mirella Lapata (2010). Topic models for image annotation and text illustration. In *Human Language Technologies: The 2010 Annual Conference of the North American Chapter of the Association for Computational Linguistics*, pp. 831–839. Association for Computational Linguistics.

Ho, Chien-Ju, Tao-Hsuan Chang, Jong-Chuan Lee, Jane Yung-Jen Hsu, and Kuan-Ta Chen (2009). KissKissBan: a competitive human computation game for image annotation. In *Proceedings of the ACM SIGKDD workshop on human computation*, pp. 11–14. ACM.

Hollink, Laura (2006). *Semantic annotation for retrieval of visual resources.* Ph. D. thesis.

Hollink, Laura, Guus Schreiber, Jan Wielemaker, Bob Wielinga, et al. (2003). Semantic annotation of image collections. In *Knowledge capture*, pp. 41–48.

[7]Features from SpatialML are already incorporated into ISOspace, and the relations in Spatial Role Labeling are captured through the relation tags in ISOspace.

Ide, N. and L. Romary (2004). International standard for a linguistic annotation framework. *Natural Language Engineering 10*(3-4), 211–225.

ISO/TC 37/SC 4/WG 2, Project leaders: James Pustejovsky, Kiyong Lee (2012). Iso 24617-1:2012 language resource management - part 1: Time and events (iso-timeml). ISO/TC 37/SC 4/WG 2.

ISO/TC 37/SC 4/WG 2, Project leaders: James Pustejovsky, Kiyong Lee (2014). Iso 24617-7:2014 language resource management - part 7: Spatial information (isospace). ISO/TC 37/SC 4/WG 2.

Karpathy, Andrej and Li Fei-Fei (2014). Deep visual-semantic alignments for generating image descriptions. *arXiv preprint arXiv:1412.2306*.

Kiros, Ryan, Ruslan Salakhutdinov, and Richard S Zemel (2014). Unifying visual-semantic embeddings with multimodal neural language models. *arXiv preprint arXiv:1411.2539*.

Klavans, J., C. Sheffield, E. Abels, J. Beaudoin, L. Jenemann, J. Lin, T. Lippincott, R. Passonneau, T. Sidhu, D. Soergel, et al. (2008). Computational Linguistics for Metadata Building: Aggregating Text Processing Technologies for Enhanced Image Access. In *OntoImage 2008: 2nd Workshop on Language Resources for Content-Based Image Retrieval, LREC*, pp. 42–46.

Kordjamshidi, Parisa, Marie-Francine Moens, and Martijn van Otterlo (2010). Spatial role labeling: Task definition and annotation scheme. In *Proceedings of the Seventh conference on International Language Resources and Evaluation (LREC'10)*, pp. 413–420.

Lee, Kiyong (2013). *Proceedings of the 9th Joint ISO - ACL SIGSEM Workshop on Interoperable Semantic Annotation*, Chapter Multi-layered Annotation of Non-textual Data for Spatial Information, pp. 15–24. Association for Computational Linguistics.

Li, Li-Jia and Li Fei-Fei (2007). What, where and who? Classifying events by scene and object recognition. In *Computer Vision, 2007. ICCV 2007. IEEE 11th International Conference on*, pp. 1–8. IEEE.

Luo, Jie, Barbara Caputo, and Vittorio Ferrari (2009). Whos doing what: Joint modeling of names and verbs for simultaneous face and pose annotation. In *Advances in Neural Information Processing Systems*, pp. 1168–1176.

Lux, Mathias (2009). Caliph & Emir: MPEG-7 photo annotation and retrieval. In *Proceedings of the 17th ACM international conference on Multimedia*, pp. 925–926. ACM.

Lux, Mathias, Jutta Becker, and Harald Krottmaier (2003). Semantic Annotation and Retrieval of Digital Photos. In *CAiSE Short Paper Proceedings*.

Lux, Mathias and Michael Granitzer (2005). Retrieval of MPEG-7 based semantic descriptions. In *BTW-Workshop "WebDB Meets IR"*, Volume 11.

Mani, Inderjeet, Christy Doran, Dave Harris, Janet Hitzeman, Rob Quimby, Justin Richer, Ben Wellner, Scott Mardis, and Seamus Clancy (2010). Spatialml: annotation scheme, resources, and evaluation. *Language Resources and Evaluation 44*, 263–280. 10.1007/s10579-010-9121-0.

Martinez, Jose Maria (2004). MPEG-7 overview (version 10), ISO. Technical report, IEC JTC1/SC29/WG11.

Nemrava, Jan, Paul Buitelaar, Vojtech Svatek, and Thierry Declerck (2008). Text mining support for semantic indexing and analysis of a/v streams. In *OntoImage 2008*. ELDA.

Pustejovsky, James (1995). *The Generative Lexicon*. Cambridge, MA: MIT Press.

Pustejovsky, James, José M Castano, Robert Ingria, Roser Sauri, Robert J Gaizauskas, Andrea Setzer, Graham Katz, and Dragomir R Radev (2003). TimeML: Robust Specification of Event and Temporal Expressions in Text. *New directions in question answering 3*, 28–34.

Pustejovsky, James, Robert Knippen, Jessica Littman, and Roser Saurí (2005, May). Temporal and event information in natural language text. *Language Resources and Evaluation 39*, 123–164.

Pustejovsky, James, Kiyong Lee, Harry Bunt, and Laurent Romary (2010). Iso-timeml: A standard for annotating temporal information in language. In *Proceedings of LREC*, pp. 394–397.

Pustejovsky, James, Jessica Moszkowicz, and Marc Verhagen (2012). A linguistically grounded annotation language for spatial information. *TAL 53*(2).

Pustejovsky, James, Jessica L Moszkowicz, and Marc Verhagen (2011). ISO-Space: The annotation of spatial information in language. In *Proceedings of the Sixth Joint ISO-ACL SIGSEM Workshop on Interoperable Semantic Annotation*, pp. 1–9.

Pustejovsky, James and Zachary Yocum (2014). Image Annotation with ISO-Space: Distinguishing Content from Structure. In N. Calzolari, K. Choukri, T. Declerck, H. Loftsson, B. Maegaard, J. Mariani, A. Moreno, J. Odijk, and S. Piperidis (eds.), *Proceedings of the Ninth International Conference on Language Resources and Evaluation (LREC'14)*, Reykjavik, Iceland. European Language Resources Association (ELRA).

Randell, David, Zhan Cui, and Anthony Cohn (1992). A spatial logic based on regions and connections. In M. Kaufmann (ed.), *Proceedings of the 3rd Internation Conference on Knowledge Representation and Reasoning*, San Mateo, pp. 165–176.

Roser, Saurí and J Pustejovsky (2008). From structure to interpretation: A double-layered annotation for event factuality. In *Proceedings of the 2nd Linguistic Annotation Workshop*.

Schuler, Karin Kipper (2005). Verbnet: A broad-coverage, comprehensive verb lexicon.

Von Ahn, Luis and Laura Dabbish (2004). Labeling images with a computer game. In *Proceedings of the SIGCHI conference on Human factors in computing systems*, pp. 319–326. ACM.

Von Ahn, Luis, Ruoran Liu, and Manuel Blum (2006). Peekaboom: a game for locating objects in images. In *Proceedings of the SIGCHI conference on Human Factors in computing systems*, pp. 55–64. ACM.

Zitnick, C Lawrence and Devi Parikh (2013). Bringing semantics into focus using visual abstraction. In *Conference on Computer Vision and Pattern Recognition (CVPR), 2013*, pp. 3009–3016. IEEE.

Factors Influencing the Implicitation of Discourse Relations across Languages

Jet Hoek*
*Utrecht Institute of Linguistics
Utrecht University, The Netherlands
j.hoek@uu.nl

Sandrine Zufferey**
**Université de Fribourg,
Switzerland
sandrine.zufferey@unifr.ch

Abstract

Relations that hold between discourse segments can, but need not, be made explicit by means of discourse connectives. Even though the explicit signaling of discourse relations is optional, not all relations can be easily conveyed implicitly. It has been proposed that readers and listeners have certain expectations about discourse and that discourse relations that are in line with these expectations (default) are more often implicit than the ones that are not (non-default). In this paper, we analyze the implicitation of discourse relations from a multilingual perspective. Using an annotation scheme for discourse relations based on Sanders, Spooren, & Noordman (1992), we distinguish between default and non-default discourse relations to predict the amount of implicit translations per relation in parallel corpora from four language pairs. We argue that the existing hypotheses about reader expectations are not sufficient to explain default discourse relations and propose that the rate of implicitation of discourse relations is governed by cognitive complexity: default discourse relations are cognitively simple within the framework of basic categories of discourse relations.

1. Introduction

Discourse connectives like *but* and *because* in English are often used to explicitly mark discourse relations such as 'cause' and 'concession' that hold between two discourse segments (Halliday & Hasan, 1976; Mann & Thompson, 1988; Sanders, Spooren, & Noordman, 1992; Knott & Dale, 1994). In addition, connectives are important for text processing, comprehension and memorization (e.g. Britton et al., 1982; Caron, Micko, & Thüring, 1988; Haberlandt, 1982; Millis, Golding, & Barker, 1995; Sanders & Noordman, 2000). Despite their usefulness, connectives are not indispensable for the communication of discourse relations, as they can often be left implicit, in which case the relation can be reconstructed by inference. The causal relation conveyed by the connective *because* in (1) can for instance still be inferred in the absence of this connective, as in (2).

(1) John is happy because he won the race.
(2) John is happy. He won the race.

Not all discourse relations, however, are equally easy to infer in the absence of a connective. For example, if the concessive connective *although* in (3) is removed, as in (4), the original coherence relation between the two segments is lost. In (4), the second segment is expected to be explaining the first one, but the semantic content of the relation clashes with this expectation, as the fact of losing the race is not a likely reason for being happy.

(3) John is happy although he lost the race.
(4) ? John is happy. He lost the race.

Sanders (2005) proposed the "causality-by-default hypothesis" for the interpretation of implicit relations, which states that hearers by default expect two segments in a discourse to be causally related. This may explain the causal interpretation triggered by the implicit relation in (4). There are, however, restrictions to this causality-by-default principle. Most importantly, the propositional content of the two segments (clauses) has to allow for a causal interpretation. Murray's (1995; 1997) "continuity hypothesis" suggests that readers by default expect each discourse segment to be both causally and temporally continuous with the preceding context. More specifically, by default, hearers expect events in discourse to correspond to the order in which they occurred in the world.

The roles of continuity and causality for discourse processing have been confirmed in a number of experimental studies. Murray (1997) found that when subjects are asked to continue a sentence ending with a period, their answers are often causally related to the first segment. Sanders & Noordman (2000) found that segments that are causally related to the preceding discourse are processed faster than when identical segments hold an additive relation to the preceding context. The causally related information was also recalled better. More recently, Kuperberg, Paczynski and Ditman (2011) demonstrated that causal inference influenced the processing of upcoming words in a sentence even in the absence of a connective. In addition, Koornneef and Sanders (2013) and Mak and Sanders (2013) show that causal expectations influence the processing of implicit relations and relations signaled by *because*, but not the processing of relations signaled by *but* or *and*.

Another line of evidence for these principles comes from corpus data. Asr and Demberg (2012; 2013) used the annotation of explicit and implicit relations provided in the Penn Discourse Tree Bank corpus (Prasad et al., 2008), starting from the assumption that connectives can be absent in expected relations. This assumption is related to the Uniform Information Density Hypothesis (Frank & Jaeger, 2008), which states that information is evenly spread across sentences within a text and that redundant markers tend to be omitted. Asr and Demberg calculated the ratio of implicitness for each coherence relation by dividing the number of implicit occurrences of a relation by its total number of occurrences. They reported that discontinuous relations such as 'concession' had indeed a lower ratio of implicitness than continuous relations like 'cause' and 'addition'. They also reported more fine-grained distinctions within categories of discourse relations. More specifically, they found that temporal relations following the order of events in the world had a higher ratio of implicitness than temporal relations reversing the order of events in the world. In short, their corpus study suggests that continuous and causal relations are expected by default, leading to a higher number of implicit relations.

Asr and Demberg's corpus studies were conducted from a monolingual perspective. An important question for the study of explicit and implicit communication of discourse relations that we investigate in this paper is whether the same principles apply cross-linguistically. We argue that if the principles that influence expectations about discourse are cognitively motivated, as they are hypothesized to be, then they should apply in the same way across languages. In order to investigate this question, we counted the number of explicit and implicit translations of several connectives conveying expected, or default, relations and connectives conveying unexpected, or non-default, relations in a large multilingual corpus. Although connectives are well known to be volatile items in translation (Halverson, 2004; Zufferey & Cartoni, 2014) and can be added, removed, or rephrased by translators, this variability should be limited by the potential of implicitness of each discourse relation. More specifically, we hypothesize that relations expressing default interpretations (i.e. continuous and causal relations) should be implicitated in translation more often than non-default relations, independently of the range of translation equivalents provided by the target language for each connective. In Section 2, we present the corpus study conducted to assess this hypothesis and we discuss its results and implications for future research in Section 3.

2. Corpus study

To test whether default relations more often receive an implicit translation than non-default relations, we extracted a set of discourse relations from the directional version of the Europarl corpus: Europarl Direct (Koehn, 2005; Cartoni, Zufferey & Meyer, 2013). Unlike the original Europarl corpus, Europarl Direct is a set of parallel corpora that only contains fragments that were originally uttered in the relevant source language, along with its corresponding translations. We selected English as our source language, and Dutch, German, French, and Spanish as our target languages: our final selection consisted of English discourse relations, with their translations in all four target languages.

As Table 1 shows, we selected discourse relations that were expressed by means of an English connective representative of certain basic features from a taxonomy of coherence relations (Sanders et al., 1992; Scholman, Evers-Vermeul, Sanders, submitted):

Connective	Relation	Continuity
Also	Positive, additive	Continuous
Because	Positive, causal	Continuous
Although	Negative, additive/causal	Discontinuous
If	Positive, conditional	?

Table 1. Basic features the English connectives prototypically convey and whether these are continuous or discontinuous.

The discourse annotation method proposed by Sanders et al. (1992) distinguishes different features of discourse relations (in addition, 'end labels,' or relations names, are provided for the relation as a whole; most discourse annotation schemes employ only relation names). One of these features is 'polarity.' A discourse relation consists of an antecedent (*P*) and a consequent (*Q*). A relation has positive polarity if the two segments, S_1 and S_2, function as *P* and *Q*, as in (1): winning a race is a plausible reason for being happy. A relation has negative polarity if *P* or *Q* is expressed by a negative counterpart of S_1 or S_2 (not-S_1 or not-S_2), as in (3): not winning a race is not likely to result in a happy contestant. Other features of discourse relations are 'basic operation' (causal, additive, temporal, conditional), 'source of coherence' (objective, subjective, speech act), and 'order of the segments' (basic (*P-Q*) non-basic(*Q-P*)). The current study only discusses the polarity and the basic operation of discourse relations.

Also and *because* both signal relations with positive polarity. *Because* is used to convey causal relations, whereas *also* signals additive, non-causal, relations. The continuity hypothesis does not predict any differences in implicitation between additive and causal relations, since both can be considered continuous relations, but based on the causality-by-default hypothesis, which poses that the default interpretation of implicit relations is a causal one, we suspect that causal relations are more often implicitated than additive relations. *Although* signals relations with negative polarity. Negative relations can be considered discontinuous: the discourse segments do not follow logically from each other. Instead, one of the segments functions as a negative counterpart to the other segment (e.g. contrastive cause – consequence). Since negative relations do not constitute a default interpretation by readers or listeners, we suspect that they will be less often translated implicitly than positive relations. Finally, we selected conditional relations, prototypically signaled by *if* in English. Although conditional relations cannot be categorized as either continuous or discontinuous, corpus-based studies demonstrate that they are almost always signaled by means of a connective (Asr & Demberg, 2012; Das & Taboada, 2013; Taboada & Das, 2013). We therefore expect to find a limited amount of implicit translations of relations signaled by *if*.

After randomly extracting fragments from the parallel corpora based on the presence of *although*, *because*, *also*, or *if*, we selected only those fragments in which the connective was used to signal a discourse relation. We then manually annotated the way in which the relations were translated: explicitly, implicitly, or by means of a paraphrase or syntactic construction. Translated fragments were only considered to be implicit discourse relations if they still contained a discourse relation. Although the meaning of (5) is very similar to (1) or (2), it cannot be considered an implicit discourse relation:

(5) His victory made John very happy.

Examples such as (5) were therefore categorized as paraphrases. Fragments categorized as syntactic constructions were for instance translations of conditional relations by means of a subjunctive in German.

3. Results and discussion

The number of implicitations per relation and target language can be found in Table 2. This includes only those translations that contained a discourse relation: all instances in which the target text used a paraphrase or syntactic construction to convey the meaning of the discourse relation in the source text were excluded from the analysis. Translations in which the meaning of the original discourse relation was lost were also left out of consideration.

	Dutch (%)	German (%)	French (%)	Spanish (%)
Also	19/194 (9.50)	15/181 (7.50)	14/190 (7.00)	7/195 (3.50)
Because	27/383 (6.37)	8/391 (1.89)	19/389 (4.48)	4/393 (0.94)
Although	7/248 (2.68)	2/248 (0.77)	5/256 (1.91)	1/261 (0.38)
If	0/226 (0.00)	0/201 (0.00)	0/222 (0.00)	0/241 (0.00)

Table 2. Number of implicitations per English connective per target language compared to the total of all discourse relations in the target text that corresponded to the original relation in the source text.

The results from Table 2 indicate that the overall rate of implicitation appears to differ between language pairs. In English-Dutch and English-French translations, for instance, a lot more relations appear implicitly in the target texts than in English-Spanish translations. This corresponds to observations from both quantitative and qualitative analyses of translations (e.g. Becher, 2011; Cartoni, Zufferey, Meyer, & Popescu-Belis, 2011). Despite the overall difference in the level of implicitation, similar relative differences between the implicitation of relations can be observed, see Tables 3a-d in the appendix for details.

As we hypothesized, in all languages positive additive relations (signaled by *also*) are translated implicitly significantly more often than negative (*although*) (all $p<0.05$) and conditional (*if*) relations (all $p<0.001$). In both Dutch and French positive causal relations (*because*) are also translated implicitly significantly more often than negative and conditional relations (all $p<0.05$), but these differences were not found for Spanish (causal vs. negative $p=0.338$, causal vs. conditional $p=0.147$). In German, we found a significant difference between causal relations and conditional relations ($p<0.05$), but not between causal relations and negative relations ($p=0.183$). A comparison between additive and causal relations indicated that there was a significant difference in implicitation in the other direction than we initially hypothesized on the basis of the causality-by-default hypothesis: in all target languages except for Dutch ($p=0.16$), we found more implicit additive relations than implicit causal relations (all $p<0.05$). Finally, we found more implicit negative relations than conditional relations in both Dutch and French (both $p<0.05$). In fact, we did not find instances of implicitated conditional relations in any of the target languages.

Although these results partly confirm our hypotheses, they seem to call for a reconsideration of the role of default interpretations, or expectations, in the implicitness of discourse relations. The causality-by-default hypothesis poses that readers expect relations to be causally related. However, it also points out that "readers will … arrive at an additive relation if no causal relation can be established" (Sanders, 2005, p. 9). The causality-by-default hypothesis rightly predicts that causal relations can often be implicit, but when applied to the implicitness of discourse relations it can conversely be interpreted as blocking the possibility of expressing an additive relation without a connective when the resulting implicit relation can be interpreted as a causal one (additive connectives have been claimed to block a causal interpretation of discourse relations, e.g. Levinson (2000), Koornneef and Sanders (2013), and Mak and Sanders (2013)). Indeed, none of the implicit additive relations in our study allow for a causal relation. Our finding that there were more implicit additive relations than causal relations in three out of four target languages might thus largely be influenced by the number of additive relations that would, when implicit, allow for a causal interpretation. We will address this question in the continuation of this study.

The hypothesis that default interpretations cannot only facilitate implicitation but also block it can be extended to the continuity hypothesis: when a relation does not constitute a default relation (either positive causal or positive additive), it can only be implicit if the content of the two segments blocks the default interpretation, or when there is enough evidence in favor of a non-default relation, for instance the presence of word pairs (e.g. Halliday and Hasan's (1976) 'semantic relations' or Taboada and Das's (2013) 'entity features'). Corroborating this hypothesis are the few conditional relations we found in our study from which the conditional connective had been removed: these can no longer be interpreted as conditional relations and instead receive a causal or additive relation. Because the relation in the target text did not correspond to the relation in the source text, we did not consider these relations to be examples of implicit conditional relations.

Our results support findings from monolingual corpus studies that conditional relations are usually explicit. Conditional relations can therefore be supposed to constitute non-default interpretations, but neither the causality-by-default hypothesis nor the continuity hypothesis can account for this. We therefore propose that default interpretations are governed by cognitive complexity. In the framework of basic features of discourse relations we employ, there are cognitively more complex members on each level: relations with negative polarity are for instance more complex than relations with positive polarity, relations with a non-basic order of segments are more complex than basic order relations, and conditional relations are more complex than non-conditional relations (see also Evers-Vermeul & Sanders, 2009). The cognitively simple alternatives then constitute the default interpretations. Note that this hypothesis makes rather fine-grained predictions, as a relation can be relatively complex or simple, default of non-default, on multiple levels. To test this hypothesis, we will continue to extend the current study by manually annotating each relation in the source language and determining the specific relation they signal within the framework of basic features.

Acknowledgments

We are grateful to the Swiss National Science Foundation (SNSF) for the funding of this work under its Sinergia program, grant n. CRSII2_147653 (MODERN project, see www.idiap.ch/project/modern/).

Appendix

Dutch

	also	*although*	*if*
because	χ^2=0.97 p=0.16	χ^2=4.48 p<0.05	χ^2=15.05 p<0.001
also		χ^2=8.34 p<0.05	χ^2=20.97 p<0.001
although			χ^2=4.68 p<0.05

Table 3a English-Dutch data

German

	also	*although*	*if*
because	χ^2=10.92 p<0.001	χ^2=0.82 p=0.183	χ^2=9.63 p<0.05
also		χ^2=13.48 p<0.001	χ^2=19.15 p<0.001
although			p=0.305*

Table 3b English-German data

French

	also	*although*	*if*
because	χ^2=2.78 p<0.05	χ^2=2.93 p<0.05	χ^2=9.63 p<0.001
also		χ^2=9.68 p<0.001	χ^2=18.21 p<0.001
although			p<0.05*

Table 3c English-French data

Spanish

	also	*although*	*if*
because	p=0.036*	p=0.338*	p=0.147*
also		p<0.05*	p<0.001*
although			p=0.520*

Table 3d English-Spanish

Tables 3a-d. Comparison of implicitation of discourse relations in the parallel corpora. All measures are Chi-square analyses (one-sided, df=1), unless marked with *: these are Fisher's exact tests (one-sided, df=1).

References

Asr, F.T. & Demberg, V. (2012). Implicitness of discourse relations. *Proceedings of COLING.* Mumbai, India.

Asr, F.T. & Demberg, V. (2013). On the information conveyed by discourse markers. *Proceedings of the Fourth Annual Workshop on Cognitive Modeling and Computational Linguistics,* 84-93. Sofia: Bulgaria.

Becher, V. (2011). When and why do translators add connectives? *Target* 23(1), 26-47.

Britton, B.K., Glynn, S.M., Meyer, B.J.F., & Penland, M..J. (1982). Effects of text structure on the use of cognitive capacity during reading. *Journal of Educational Psychology* 74, 51–61.

Caron, J., Micko, H.C., & Thuring, M. (1988). Conjunctions and the recall of composite sentences. *Journal of Memory and Language* 27, 309–323.

Cartoni, B., Zufferey, S., & Meyer, T. (2013). Using the Europarl corpus for linguistics research. *Belgian Journal of Linguistics* 27, 23-42.

Cartoni, B., Zufferey, S., Meyer, T., & Popescu-Belis, A. (2011). How comparable are parallel corpora? Measuring the distribution of general vocabulary and connectives. *Proceedings of the 4th Workshop on Building and Using Comparable Corpora*, 78-86. Portland, Oregon.

Das, D. & Taboada, M. (2013). Explicit and implicit coherence relations: A corpus study. *Proceedings of the 2013 annual conference of the Canadian Linguistic Association.*

Evers-Vermeul, J. & Sanders, T.J.M. (2009). The emergence of Dutch connectives; how cumulative cognitive complexity explains the order of acquisition. *Journal of Child Language* 36(4), 829-854.

Frank, A. & Jaeger, T. (2008). Speaking rationally: Uniform information density as an optimal strategy for language production. *Proceedings of the 28th meeting of the Cognitive Science Society*.

Haberlandt, K. (1982). Reader expectations in text comprehension. In: J-F Le Ny & W Kintsch (Eds.), *Language and Comprehension*. North-Holland, Amsterdam, 239-249.

Halliday, M.A.K. & Hasan, R. (1976). *Cohesion in English.* Longman, London.

Halverson, S. (2004). Connectives as a translation problem. In: H. Kittel et al. (Eds.), *An International Encyclopedia of Translation Studies*, 562–572. Berlin/New York: Walter de Gruyter.

Knott, A. & Dale, R. (1994). Using linguistic phenomena to motivate a set of coherence relations. *Discourse Processes* 18, 35–62.

Koehn, P. (2005) Europarl: A parallel corpus for statistical machine translation. *Proceedings of the 10th Machine Translation Summit*, 79-86. Phuket, Thailand.

Koornneef, A.W., & Sanders, T.J.M. (2013). Establishing coherence relations in discourse: The influence of implicit causality and connectives on pronoun resolution. *Language and Cognitive Processes* 28(8), 1169-1206.

Kuperberg, G., Paczynski, M., and Ditman, T. (2011). Establishing causal coherence across sentences: An ERP study. *Journal of Cognitive Neuroscience* 23, 1230–1246.

Mak, W.M., Sanders, T.J.M. (2013). The role of causality in discourse processing: Effects of expectation and coherence relations. *Language and Discourse Processes* 28(9), 1414-1437.

Mann, W.C., & Thompson, S.A. (1988). Rhetorical structure theory: Toward a functional theory of text organization. *Text* 8, 243–281.

Millis, K.K., Golding, J.M., & Barker, G. (1995). Causal connectives increase inference generation. *Discourse Processes* 20(1), 29–49.

Murray, J.D. (1995). Logical connectives and local coherence. In R. Lorch & E. O'Brien (Eds.), *Sources of cohesion in text comprehension*, 107-125. Hillsdale, NJ: Erlbaum.

Murray, J.D. (1997). Connectives and narrative text: The role of continuity. *Memory and Cognition* 25, 227–236.

Prasad, R., Dinesh, N., Lee, A., Miltsakaki, E., Robaldo, L., Joshi, A., & Webber, B. (2008). The Penn Discourse Treebank 2.0. *Proceedings of the 6th International Conference on Language Resources and Evaluation* (LREC 2008), 2961–2968.

Sanders, T.J.M. (2005). Coherence, causality and cognitive complexity in discourse. *Proceedings/Actes SEM-05, First International Symposium on the Exploration and Modelling of Meaning,* 105–114.

Sanders, T.J.M., & Noordman, L.G.M. (2000). The role of coherence relations and their linguistic markers in text processing. *Discourse Processes* 29, 37–60.

Sanders T.J.M., Spooren W.P.M.S. & Noordman L.G.M. (1992). Towards a Taxonomy of Coherence Relations. *Discourse Processes* 15, 1–36.

Scholman, M.C.J., Evers-Vermeul, J., & Sanders, T.J.M. (subm.). *Categories of coherence relations in discourse annotation*. Submitted for publication.

Taboada, M. & Das, D. (2013). Annotation upon annotation: Adding signalling information to a corpus of discourse relations. *Dialogue and Discourse* 4(2), 249–281.

Zufferey, S. & Cartoni, B. (2014). A multifactorial analysis of explicitation in translation. *Target* 26, 361–384.

Instrument subjects without Instrument role

Elisabetta Ježek
Università di Pavia
jezek@unipv.it

Rossella Varvara
CIMeC - Università di Trento
rossella.varvara@unitn.it

Abstract

Large-scale linguistic resources that provide relational information about predicates and their arguments are indispensable tools for a wide rage of NLP applications, where the participants of a certain event expressed by a predicate need to be detected. In particular, hand-annotated corpora combining semantic and syntactic information constitute the backbone for the development of probabilistic models that automatically identify the semantic relationships conveyed by sentential constituents in text, as in the case of Semantic Role Labeling (Gildea and Jurafsky, 2002). Even if attempts of standardization of semantic role annotations are being developed (cf. the LIRICS project, Petukhova and Bunt 2008), controversial points are still present. In this paper we examine a problematic semantic role, the Instrument role, which presents differences in definition and causes problems of attribution. Particularly, it is not clear whether to assign this role to inanimate entities occurring as subjects or not. This problem is especially relevant 1- because of its treatment in practical annotation and semantic role labeling, 2- because it affects the whole definition of semantic roles. We propose that inanimate nouns denoting instruments in subject positions are not instantiations of the Instrument role, but are Cause, Agent or Theme. Ambiguities in the annotation of these cases are due to confusion between semantic roles and ontological types associated with event participants.

1 Introduction

Semantically annotated resources have become widely used and requested in the field of Natural Language Processing, growing as a productive research area. This trend can be confirmed by looking at the repeated attempts in the implementation of annotated resources (FrameNet - Fillmore et al. 2002, VerbNet - Kipper-Schuler 2005, Propbank - Palmer et al. 2005, SALSA - Burchardt et al.2006) and in the task of automatic Semantic Role Labeling (Gildea and Jurafsky 2002, Surdeanu et al. 2007, Màrquez et al. 2008, Lang and Lapata 2010, Titov and Klementiev 2012 among others).

Since their first introduction by Fillmore (1967), semantic roles have been described and defined in many different ways, with different sets and different level of granularity - from macro-roles (Dowty 1991) to frame-specific ones (Fillmore et al. 2002). In order to reach a common standard in terms of number and definition, the LIRICS (Linguistic Infrastructure for Interoperable ResourCes and Systems) project has recently evaluated several approaches for semantic role annotation and proposed an ISO (International Organization for Standardization) ratified standard (ISO 2013).

In this paper we examine a problematic issue in semantic role attribution. We focus on a single role, the Instrument role, whose definition and designation should be, in our opinion, reconsidered. The topic is particularly relevant since its treatment in different lexical resources is not homogeneous and the theoretical debate is still lively. Moreover, this issue highlights aspects of the nature of semantic roles, relevant both for their theoretical definition and for practical annotation, such as the difference between semantic roles and ontological types. The former refer to the role of participants in the particular event described by the linguistic expression, the latter to the inherent properties of the entities. We argue that despite the availability of different sets of tags for roles and types in lexical resources such as Framenet and VerbNet, roles (Instruments in particular) and types are still often confused.

2 Background

The analysis arises from the enrichment of the *Senso Comune* knowledge base of the Italian language (henceforth SC) (Vetere et al. 2012) with semantic role sets for predicates, to be used for linguistic research and NLP applications. In SC semantic roles sets are not assigned to predicate structures axiomatically but they are induced by the annotation of the usage examples associated with the *sensi fondamentali* (word meanings which are predominant in terms of use among the most frequent 2000 words in the language, cf. De Mauro, 1999) of the verb lemmas. The target corpus consists of about 8000 usage examples. Up to now we annotated about 6 % of the entire corpus in a pilot experiment we performed to release the beta version of the annotation scheme (details in Ježek et al. 2014). The methodology encompasses annotation of the role played by participants in the event described by the predicate (intentional agent, affected entity, created entity and so on) as well as annotation of their inherent semantic properties, expressed in the form of ontological categories (person, substance, artifact, and so forth) organized in a taxonomy. The dataset we focus here was composed of 66 examples without disambiguation, 3 each for 22 target verbs, and it was annotated for semantic roles by 8 annotators. Annotators were instructed with a guideline in which a set of 24 coarse-grained (high level) roles was defined, with examples and a taxonomy, based on LIRICS (Petukhova and Bunt 2008) and subsequent related work (Bonial et al. 2011 a, b). In designing the set, some LIRICS roles such as Agent and Partner (Co-Agent in VerbNet) were conflated, and some classical semantic roles like Experiencer rather than LIRICS's ambiguous Pivot were used. The final set of roles for SC is given in Table 1, together with the mappings with the ISO roles of LIRICS.

SensoComune role	**LIRICS role**
Agente (AG)	Agent, Partner
Causa (CAUSE)	Cause, Reason
Strumento (INSTR)	Instrument, Means
Paziente (PT)	Patient
Tema (TH)	Theme, Pivot
Goal (GOAL)	Goal
Beneficiario (BEN)	Beneficiary
Origine (SOURCE)	Source
Luogo (LOC)	Location, Setting
LuogoFinale (ENDLOC)	EndLocation
LuogoIniziale (INITLOC)	InitialLocation
Percorso (PATH)	Path
Distanza (DIST)	Distance
Tempo (TIME)	Time
TempoFinale (ENDTIME)	EndTime
TempoIniziale (INITTIME)	InitialTime
Durata (DUR)	Duration
Risultato (RESULT)	Result
Quantità (AMOUNT)	Amount
Maniera (MANNER)	Manner, Medium
Esperiente (EXP)	Pivot, Patient
Scopo (PURPOSE)	Purpose
Frequenza (FREQ)	Frequency
Attributo (ATTR)	Attribute

Table 1: Semantic roles set

As referenced above, each role in SC is defined by a gloss and a set of examples, in the LIRICS style.

During the evaluation process, the major cases of disagreement were highlighted. The present study is based on the evidence coming from these data; the Instrument role caused several misunderstandings (see also Varvara 2013). Nevertheless, our analysis will look primarily at examples from literature and other resources in order to rethink this role and to reach a standardization. We propose to consider what are called instrument subjects (Alexiadou and Schäfer 2006) as instances of three different roles, namely

Cause, Agent and Theme, rather than as Instrument. In the following, we first define instrument subjects (section 2) and highlight the problems that arise in the assignment of the Instrument role to these cases (section 3), then we provide examples and arguments that support our proposal (section 3.1-3.3). We conclude by highlighting the mutual dependence between theoretical analysis and practical annotation.

3 The case of instrument subjects

With "instrument subjects" we refer to examples in which a noun, denoting an inanimate entity frequently used as instrument by humans (and occurring in *with*-phrases), is the subject of the sentence, as in the examples below (Levin 1993:80, Schlesinger 1989:189):

(1) "**The hammer** broke the window."

(2) "**The stick** hit the horse."

It has been frequently asserted that these subjects cover the role of Instrument (Fillmore 1967, Nilsen 1973, Dowty 1991), similarly to the nouns preceded by the preposition *with* in (3) and (4); in Levin (1993)'s terms, these are called "Instrument-Subject alternation" [1].

(3) "David broke the window **with a hammer**."

(4) "Marvin hit the horse **with a stick**."

Several authors have argued against the interpretation of Instrument subjects as Instrument roles, suggesting other roles to these cases (Schlesinger 1989, DeLancey 1991, Van Valin and Wilkins 1996, Alexiadou and Schäfer 2006, Grimm 2013, among others). Their basic claim is that the class of instrument subjects does not correspond to the class of instruments occurring in *with-phrases*. Nevertheless, also in the implementation of lexical resources the trend is still to consider instrument subjects as instances of the Instrument role. In Verbnet, for example, instrument subjects are tagged with the role Instrument, as can be seen in the annotation of the verb *hit*:

(5) "**The stick** hit the fence."

(6) "**The hammer** hit the window to pieces."

(7) "**The stick** hit the door open".

In the LIRICS guidelines (Schiffrin and Bunt 2007:38) the Instrument-Subject alternation is used as exemplification of the definition of the Instrument role: "He opened the door [with the key (Instrument)]"; "[The brick (Instrument)] hit the window and shattered it." The reason of the annotation of these last examples is not clear if we look at the role definition (as annotators usually do). In the guidelines, the Instrument is defined as the "participant in an event that is manipulated by an agent, and with which an intentional act is performed" (2007:38). In the definition, the agent and the intentionality of the act are explicitly mentioned, but while annotating examples such as the ones above a question arises: in order to tag a noun phrase with the role Instrument, should the Agent be linguistically expressed, could it be just inferable or even totally absent?

[1] The term "instrument subject" is used by many to cover also other Levin's alternations, such as Characteristic property alternation (1993:39) or Middle alternation (1993:26). Even the examples that will be a matter of discussion in the present study can be ascribed to different alternations. We will then use the term "instrument subject" in a broad sense, taking into account every noun that can occur both in a *with*-phrase and in subject position. Even if this term may cause confusion with the true semantic role Instrument, we will adopt it because of lack of other appropriate terms. To avoid difficulties, we will use the capital initial letter for semantic roles and the lower initial for the words used in their common sense (e.g. Agent vs agent).

4 Why instrument subjects do not perform the Instrument role

Nowadays it is a shared opinion that semantic roles are relational notions that express the role of participants in the event expressed by the verb. As pointed out by Pethukova and Bunt (2008), semantic roles should be defined not as primitives "but rather as relational notions that link participants to an event, and describe the way the participant is involved in an event, rather than by internal properties"(2008:40). We follow this line of reasoning but in addition, we claim that semantic roles should be considered as qualities attributed to participants considering their role not only in the particular event, but more specifically in the way the event is encoded syntactically and semantically in the language. Particularly, we claim that in order to assign the Instrument role, an Agent should not only be present in the event in the world, but it should be specified in the event representation reported by the predicate and be linguistically expressed. We argue that in the presence of instrument subjects, this condition is not satisfied. There is not another participant expressed as playing the Agent role; and even if an Agent is not expressed but inferrable from the previous context, the instrument subject does not play the Instrument role. In linguistic expressions with instrument subjects, it is clear that there are reasons for which speakers left the intentional Agent out of the scope of their utterance. Their intention could be to describe the instrument noun as an autonomous entity, as the only known source of causation, not as an Instrument manipulated by an Agent, and as such its role in the event should be considered.

Consider again the following example of Instrument-Subject alternation, in the light of what we just said: "The janitor opened the lock *with a key*" and "*The key* opened the lock". As referenced above, it is frequently asserted that the arguments in italics express the same semantic roles in both sentences. "The underlying argument is that since "*the key*" in 19 (the first example) is an Instrument, and since 19 and 20 could refer to the same scenario, "*the key*" must be Instrument in 20 (the second example) as well" (DeLancey 1991:348). In line with Delancey, we argue that this is an unfounded idea. The same event can be the object of two different sentences that represent the event from different perspectives and the instrumental noun can not stand in both contexts as Instrument role. In the words of DeLancey (1991:350): "case roles, like any other semantic categories, encode construals of events rather than objective facts". We believe that, looking at corpus data, it appears clearly that subjects like "the key" are not usually represented as an instrument used by an human, but as a Cause that substitutes for an unknown Agent in the causal chain (as in the previous example) or as an entity (a Theme) whose characteristic is described (e.g. the property of opening a lock in an example such as "This key opens the lock"). As referenced in the Introduction, our proposal is that instrument subjects usually cover the role of Cause, Theme or, metaphorically or metonymically, Agent. In the next sections, we will list and group into classes the occurrences of instrument subjects that we have encountered in our data, according to our proposal.

4.1 Instrument subject as Cause

Most frequently instrument subjects cover the role of Cause[2]. It is usually the case when: 1- it is not possible to find an Agent or general causer other than the instrument inanimate subject; 2- it is possible to imagine an Agent that has "activated" the inanimate entity, but it is no longer present in the scene or it is not known. This could be a choice of the speaker that does not want to include or talk about the Agent or it could be the case with generic events with non specific agents. Consider the example:

(8) "**The clock** was ticking so loudly that it woke the baby" (DeLancey 1991: 347)

It is not possible to find another participant causing the event other than the clock. The same can be seen in this sentence taken from the corpus ItTenTen (Jakubček et al. 2013):

(9) "Un masso caduto da una galleria ha messo fuori uso la metro. **Il sasso** ha rotto il pantografo, l'antenna che trasmette l'energia al treno, e ha interrotto la tensione per 600 metri di linea aerea."

[2]The definition of the role Cause in SC is the following: "participant (animate or inanimate) in an event that starts the event, but does not act intentionally; it exists independently from the event".

'A stone falling down from a tunnel put the metro out of order. **The stone** has broken the pantograph, the spar that transmits the energy to the train, and it has interrupted the tension for 600 meters.'

The stone is a Cause because nobody has thrown it, but it has taken its own energy by its falling.[3] The same interpretation could be applicable to the sentence cited before from the LIRICS guidelines "The brick hit the window and shattered it"; from this context we do not know if there is an agent that has thrown the brick; if we do not have evidence about that, we cannot consider "the brick" an Instrument in this sentence.

There are cases in which our real-world knowledge enables us to understand that the instrument subject has been manipulated by somebody, but it has been focused on in the sentence as the principal or the only known element of the causal chain[4]:

(10) "**The poison** killed its victim."

(11) "**The camomile** cured the patient".

There is a case of this sort in the dataset of the SC's annotation experiment. The subject of the sentence

(12) "**Leggi** che colpiscono il contrabbando."
'**Laws** that hit the smuggling.'

has been tagged by 2 annotators upon 8 as Instrument role instantiation; it is possible that they have thought that there was an inferred Agent (the legislator) that was using the laws as an instrument.

This kind of interpretation can emerge also with instrumental nouns not occurring as subjects. During the annotation experiment, the argument in bold in the example

(13) "l'aereo è stato colpito **da un missile**"
'the airplane was hit **by a missile**'

was tagged as Instrument by 6 upon 8 annotators. In our opinion this is a case of the role Cause rather than Instrument; it is introduced by the preposition *da* (english "by") that is usually associated with the expression of Agents and Causes in passive constructions. It can be inferred that somebody has used the missile as a means to hit the airplane, but the speaker of this sentence does not provide evidence about this eventuality. The same scenario can be expressed with an Instrument role by using a sentence like "l'aereo è stato colpito dai nemici con un missile" ('the airplane was hit by enemies with a missile'), in which the preposition "with" overtly expresses the Instrument.

It is true that there are differences in the nature of the entities that we encountered so far expressed as instrument subject. A missile is different in nature from a stone. The first is an artifact, while the second is a natural object. Moreover, from our world-knowledge, we know that the first is more frequently used intentionally than the second one. A missile is less likely to be activated accidentally than a stone, also because, in Pustejovsky's (1995) terms, it has in its telic quale the goal of being shot (to attack). Nevertheless, in our opinion, these characteristics and differences are inherent properties of the entities described, that could be relevant in the definition of an ontology of instruments, but they do not emerge in semantic role structure. Such an ontological distinction has been recognized by various scholars, such as Nilsen (1973), Kamp and Rossdeutscher (1994:144-145) among others. Kamp and Rossdeutscher proposed to distinguish a class of *Instrument Causers*, i.e. "Instruments which can be conceived as acting on their own, once the agent has applied or introduced them", from *Pure Instruments*, defined as "Instruments whose action is conceived as strictly auxiliary to that of the agent by whom they are being

[3]A reviewer pointed out that the real Cause is the event of falling, not the stone. Although this is a true inference, we argue that the stone is metonymically reinterpreted as the falling of the stone and for this reason the cause of the event. This interesting matter deserves a deeper analysis that will be subject of further work.

[4]Alexiadou and Schäfer note: "They are Causers by virtue of their being involved in an event without being (permanently) controlled by a human Agent. The fact that this involvement in an event might be the result of a human agent having introduced these Causers is a fact about the real world, not about the linguistic structure" (2006: 42-43).

employed". This is of course a correct distinction, which could lead us to classify mechanical devices (such as *clock*) and natural forces as Instrument Causers, but again this would be only an ontological classification. These differences may, of course, have interfered during the annotation.

As referenced above, we claim that even if an Agent is expressed in the previous context, the instrument subject should not be considered as Instrument. To better explain this position, consider the example in (14), kindly brought to our attention by a reviewer:

(14) "She swung at the charging wolf *with her broom*. Luckily **the broom** caught the wolf's throat and succeeded in pushing him back."

We claim that in the first sentence, the *broom* is a real Instrument, since it is described as being manipulated by somebody. In the second sentence, *the broom* as instrument subject plays no more an Instrument role, but is a Cause, since the predicate *caught* does not describe the event of the broom being used, but the event of the broom's catching the throat of the wolf. In other words, in the second sentence, the speaker highlights only the intermediate part of the causal chain. An event can be described in various ways, focusing on its parts in a narrow or wide way. For example, we can just say "I broke the window", describing only the initial and the endpoint, or we can say "I took a stone, I raised my arm, I applied all my strenght to my arm, lowered my arm and the force applied to the stone broke the window", explicitly expressing all the sub-events that compose the main event [5]. Saying that "The stone broke the window" or that "The broom caught the wolf's throat" means to focus a part of the causal chain and to represent it as the Cause. It is important to note that it is the predicate (choosen by the speaker) that provides which part of the chain is represented as the Cause. Indeed, every events can be subdivided in different sub-parts, but it depends on the specific sentence that is used which part is linguistically described.

4.2 Instrument subject as Agent

We argue that the cases in which an instrument subject covers the role of Agent are sporadic and involve metaphorical or metonymical interpretations (Jezek et al. 2014). It should be kept in mind that it is widely assumed that the Agent role implies animacy and intentionality; as such an inanimate entity like an instrument cannot be Agent. This view contrasts with what has been claimed by some linguists (Schlesinger 1989, Alexiadou and Schäfer 2006) that, while agreeing that the Instrument role attribution to instrument subjects is incorrect, claimed that in most cases they are Agents. We claim that the Agent role can be fulfilled by instrument subjects in case of personification or metaphorical/metonymic extension of the meaning of the lexeme:

(15) "Un giorno **una forbice gigante** tagliò della carta a forma di burattino. Un altro giorno ha ritagliato due palle giganti che erano il sole giallo e la Terra."
'Once upon a time a giant scissor cut a paper into a puppet. Later, it cut two giant balls, the yellow sun and the Earth.'

(16) "**Tante penne** scrivono su Napoli, usano Napoli per vendere copie."
'**A lot of pens** (writers) write about Naples, they use Naples to sell.'

(17) "**Tutto l'ufficio** ha lavorato bene."
'**All the office** has worked well.'

4.3 Instrument subject as Theme

Analyzing the SC dataset, a case has been found that to our knowledge has not been previously discussed systematically in the literature on semantic roles. The following are examples:

(18) "**La penna** scrive nero."
'**The pen** writes black.'

[5] For similar ideas see Talmy 1996.

(19) "**Forbici** che tagliano bene."
'**Scissors** that cut well.'

These subjects have been tagged as Instrument by respectively 3/8 and 4/8 annotators. As previously claimed, the ambiguity is caused by the possibility of these nouns to occur as true Instruments with the preposition "*with*" (ex. "I have written the letter with this pen"). We suggest that in cases such as (18) and (19) the instrument subjects are neither Instrument, nor Cause, because they are not presented as causing an event or as being used by an expressed Agent. The verb predicates a property of the subject and as such the Theme role is fulfilled. The Theme is defined in SC as "participant in an event or state, which, if in an event, it is essential for it to take place, but it does not determine the way in which the event happens (it doesn't have control) and it is not structurally modified by it; if in a state, it is characterized by being in a certain condition or position throughout the state and it is essential to its occurring". In other resources, these examples could be referred to by roles similar to our Theme, such as the role Pivot in LIRICS.

These cases can be ascribed to the class of *gnomic imperfective* proposed by Bertinetto and Lenci (2010). These sentences express a generalization of some kind with a characterizing function; they ascribe a defining property to the intended referent. This brings the examples in (18) and (19) to be partly similar to other habituals like "John smokes" or "John smokes cigars", defined by Bertinetto and Lenci (2010) as *attitudinal*. However, even if they both denote a state and they both ascribe a characteristic to the referent, we argue that they are intrinsically different: a sentence like "this pen writes black" or "this knife cuts meat" denotes an inherent property of the referent and its aspect can be defined as *potential*. This does not hold for attitudinals; we cannot say "John can smoke cigars" to mean that John usually smokes cigars. This is a property that John acquires by iteration of smoking events, i.e. as a result of a series of intentional acts. By contrast, the property of writing black is provided by how a pen is built, not by the fact of having participated repeatedly in the act of writing black. It is an inherent property that cannot be intentionally controlled.

5 Conclusions and future work

In this paper we have shown how theoretical and data analysis can mutually improve each other. Theoretical literature offers critical discussion about the Instrument role and the case of instrument subjects. The discussion can be useful for the definition and annotation of semantic roles in the implementation of lexical resources. Moreover, the analysis of annotated data can reveal fallacies in the reliability of the set, coming back from application to theoretical topics.

We claim that semantic roles should be assigned considering the specific linguistic encoding of the event, not the event itself. The same scenario, indeed, can be represented by more than one linguistic expression, in which the same participant can cover different roles.

At last, our study highlights the importance of distinguishing between semantic roles - relational notions belonging to the level of linguistic representation - and ontological types, which refer to internal qualities of entities. We believe that this topic is still not well understood and deserves detailed case studies on single roles at the interface between linguistic theory and data analysis, as the one presented here.

A problematic point that we leave open for future work is the amount of context that should be provided to annotators. Is it better to tag single sentences, as we did, or should the context be expanded with previous text? Future annotation experiments could shed light on this point. However, the problems highlighted in this paper about the definition of semantic roles holds anyway. It is our duty to explicitly clarify and agree on how do we interpret semantic roles (Instrument roles particularly), before asking annotators for high agreement on segmented portions of text or larger linguistic units.

Acknowledgments

Thanks to Guido Vetere, Laure Vieu, Fabio Massimo Zanzotto, Alessandro Oltramari and Aldo Gangemi for the ongoing collaborative work on semantic role annotation within the SC initiative. An earlier and shorter version of the paper was published in the Proceedings of the 1st Italian Conference on Computational Linguistics (CLIC-it, Dec. 8-10, Pisa, Italy). We acknowledge all anonymous reviewers for their very useful comments and suggestions.

References

Alexiadou, A. and F. Schäfer. 2006. Instrument subjects are agents or causers. *The Oxford Handbook of Tense and Aspect*, vol.25

Bertinetto, P. M., and Lenci, A. 2012. Habituality, pluractionality, and imperfectivity. *Proceedings of West Coast Conference on Formal Linguistics*, Oxford University Press, Oxford, 852-880.

Bonial, C., S.W. Brown, W. Corvey, V. Petukhova, M. Palmer, H. Bunt. 2011a. An Exploratory Comparison of Thematic Roles in VerbNet and LIRICS. *In Proceedings of the Sixth Joint ISO - ACL SIGSEM Workshop on Interoperable Semantic Annotation.*

Bonial, C., W. Corvey, M. Palmer, V. Petukhova, H. Bunt. 2011b. A hierarchical unification of LIRICS and VerbNet semantic roles. *In Proceedings of the 2011 IEEE Fifth International Conference on Semantic Computing*, IEEE Computer Society Washington, DC, USA, 483-489.

Burchardt, A., E. Katrin, A. Frank, A. Kowalski, S.Padó, M. Pinkal. 2006. The salsa corpus: a german corpus resource for lexical semantics. *Proceedings of LREC 2006*

DeLancey, S. 1991. Event construal and case role assignment. *Proceedings of the Annual Meeting of the Berkeley Linguistics Society*, vol.17

De Mauro, T. 1999. Introduzione. In De Mauro T. (Ed. in Chief), Grande Dizionario Italiano dellUso (GRADIT), 6 voll. + CD-rom *Torino, UTET*, vol. I, VI-XLII.

Dowty, D. 1991. Thematic proto-roles and argument selection. *Language*, 126: 547-619

Fillmore, C.J. 1967. The case for case. *Universals in Linguistic Theory*, Bach and Harms (eds). New York, Holt, Rinehart and Winston edition.

Fillmore, C. J., C. F. Baker and H. Sato. 2002. The framenet database and software tools. *Proceedings of the Third International Conference on Language Resources and Evaluation*, vol.4

Gildea, D. and D. Jurafsky 2002. Automatic labeling of semantic roles. *Computational Linguistics*, 28(3):245288.

Grimm, S. 2013. The Bounds of Subjecthood: Evidence from Instruments. *Proceedings of the 33rd Meeting of the Berkeley Linguistic Society.*,Berkeley Linguistic Society.

Jakubiček, M., Kilgarriff, A., Kovář, V., Rychlý, P., Suchomel, V. 2013. The TenTen Corpus Family *Proceedings of the International Conference on Corpus Linguistics.*

Ježek, E., Vieu L., Zanzotto F.M., Vetere G., Oltramari A., Gangemi A., Varvara R. 2014. Extending 'Senso Comune' with Semantic Role Sets. *Proceedings 10th Joint ISO - ACL SIGSEM Workshop on Interoperable Semantic Annotation*, LREC 2014.

Kamp, H. and A. Rossdeutscher 1994. Remarks on lexical structure and DRS construction. *Theoretical Linguistics*, 20:97-164.

Kipper Schuler. 2005 VerbNet: A Broad-coverage, Comprehensive Verb Lexicon. *PhD dissertation, University of Pennsylvania, Philadelphia, PA.*

ISO 2013. Language resource management - Semantic annotation framework - Part 5: Semantic Roles (SemAFSR). ISO 24617-5. Geneva: ISO Central Secretariat.

Lang, J., and Lapata, M. 2010. Unsupervised induction of semantic roles. *Human Language Technologies: The 2010 Annual Conference of the North American Chapter of the Association for Computational Linguistics*, 939-947.

Levin, B. 1993. *English verb classes and alternations: A preliminary investigation.* University of Chicago press Chicago, IL.

Màrquez, L., Carreras, X., Litkowski, K. C., and Stevenson, S. 2008. Semantic role labeling: an introduction to the special issue. *Computational linguistics*, 34(2), 145-159.

Nilsen, Don L. F. 1973. *The instrumental case in english: syntactic and semantic considerations.* The Hague; Paris: Mouton.

Palmer, M., D. Gildea, P. Kingsbury 2005. The Proposition Bank: A Corpus Annotated with Semantic Roles. *Computational Linguistics Journal, 31:1*

Pustejovsky, J. 1995. *The Generative Lexicon.* Cambridge Mass: The MIT Press.

Petukhova, V. and Bunt, H.C. 2008. LIRICS semantic role annotation: Design and evaluation of a set of data categories. *Proceedings of the Sixth International Conference on Language Resources and Evaluation (LREC 2008)*, Marrakech, Morocco, 2830.

Schiffrin, A. and Bunt, H.C. 2007. LIRICS Deliverable D4.3. Documented compilation of semantic data categories. *http://lirics.loria.fr.*.

Schlesinger, I.M. 1989. Instruments as agents: on the nature of semantic relations. *Journal of Linguistics*, 25(01). 189-210.

Surdeanu, M., L. Màrquez, X. Carreras, and P. R. Comas. 2007. Combination strategies for semantic role labeling. *Journal of Artificial Intelligence Research (JAIR)*, 29:105-151.

Talmy, l. 1996. The windowing of attention in language. *Grammatical constructions: Their form and meaning*, Shibatani and Thompson (eds), 235-287. Oxford: Oxford University Press.

Titov, I., and Klementiev, A. 2012. A Bayesian approach to unsupervised semantic role induction. *Proceedings of the 13th Conference of the European Chapter of the Association for Computational Linguistics*, pp.12-22. Association for Computational Linguistics.

Van Valin, R. D. and D. P. Wilkins. 1996. The case for "effector": case roles, agents, and agency revisited. *Grammatical constructions: Their form and meaning.*, eds. Shibatani and Thompson, 289322. Oxford: Oxford University Press.

Varvara, R. 2013. *I ruoli tematici: Agente, Strumento e la nozione di causa.* Master thesis. University of Pavia.

Vetere, G., A. Oltramari, I. Chiari, E. Jezek, L. Vieu, F.M. Zanzotto. 2012. 'Senso Comune': An Open Knowledge Base for Italian. *Revue TAL (Traitement Automatique des Langues), Journal Special Issue on Free Language Resources*, 52.3, 217-43.

The Annotation of Measure Expressions in ISO Standards

Kiyong Lee
Korea University, Seoul
ikiyong@gmail.com

Abstract

In annotating measure expressions such as *three days* and *about 123 km*, two recently published ISO standards, ISO-TimeML (ISO, 2012b) and ISOspace (ISO, 2014a), show some inconsistencies, as pointed out in ISO SemAF Principles (ISO, 2014c), a third ISO standards on semantic annotation to be published soon. Other than terminological or semantic inconsistencies introduced in ISO SemAF Principles, there are some formal inconsistencies between or within these standards. This paper attempts to resolve such inconsistencies by proposing some minimally possible modifications into the annotation schemes of those two standards. Despite these modifications, the interoperability between these standards is preserved, each retaining its own annotation scheme for either temporal or spatial information involving measures. An attempt is also made to partially merge ISO-TimeML and ISOspace as a step towards the integration of ISO SemAF standards into a modularly usable general annotation scheme for the semantic annotation of language.

1 Introduction

Measure expressions such as *three days* and *about 123km* are ubiquitous in language. Here is a short travel log which contains these measure expressions.[1]

(1) Travel Log
We flew to Toronto by Air Canada and drove to Niagara Falls **three days** *before Christmas Day. Niagara Falls is* **approximately 130 km (80 miles)** *southwest of Toronto,* **an average drive of one and a half hours** *without traffic delays. According to Google maps, Niagara is* **about 123km (76 miles)** *from Pearson Airport and it takes* **nearly 1 hour and a half** *using highways having* **speed limits of 100km/h**. *We had estimated it would take* **2 hours maximum** *and hoped to get to Niagara before 6:00 pm, but arrived at the hotel in Niagara after 10:30 pm. We had to drive for* **more than 6 hours** *because of an unexpected heavy snow storm. We drove at* **an average speed of around 20 kilometers per hour**. *We moved* **so slow**, *consuming* **so many hours** *on the road, that Niagara seemed* **very far**. *We stopped for coffee after barely driving* **50km** *(a little over 30 miles)* from Pearson Airport.

The words or strings of words in boldface refer to quantities or amounts, called *measures*.[2] Some of them refer to time amounts and others to spatial measures of various dimensions such as distances. Two of them refer to speed limits that involve a spatio-temporal dimension. Some expressions (e.g., *2 hours*) are then quantitatively explicit and others (e.g., *so many hours*) are not.

For the purpose of language resource management, an ISO Working Group[3] on semantic annotation recently published two ISO international standards, ISO-TimeML (ISO, 2012b)[4] and ISOspace (ISO, 2014a)[5]. Parts of these standards treat measure expressions, spatial and temporal, while specifying how

[1]Copied from <http://www.tripadvisor.com/Travel-g155019-c97995/Toronto:Ontario:Niagara.Falls.A.Side.Trip.From.Toronto.html> and slightly modified to suit our needs.

[2]The temporal expressions *6:00 pm* and *10:30 pm* are not in boldface because they do not refer to durations or amounts of time, but points in time.

[3]ISO/TC 37/SC 4 (Language Resource Management)/WG 2 (Semantic Annotation)

[4]Based on TimeML developed by Branimir et al. (2005), Pustejovsky et al. (2005) with some modifications which were discussed in Pustejovsky et al. (2010).

[5]Based on MITRE (2009)'s SpatialML and the Spatial Annotation Scheme developed by the Brandeis Working Group headed by James Pustejvosky. See Pustejovsky et al. (2011) and Pustejovsky et al. (2012).

to relate events (motions), paths, and some other basic entities to these measure expressions. Meanwhile, ISO SemAF Principles (ISO, 2014c)[6], a third ISO standard on semantic annotation soon to be published, has pointed out some inconsistencies between the treatments of measure expressions by these two published standards and their inadequacies as semantic annotation.

Lee (2012) had earlier argued for the merging of ISO-TimeML and ISOspace into a unified annotation scheme, especially based on functional similarities of spatial and temporal signals (e.g., various prepositions in English) that trigger the anchoring of events, motions, durations, and paths to times and locations. In this paper, we may still opt for a partial merging of these two standards by removing any inconsistencies, especially formal inconsistencies to be described in Section 3 but puts its focus on the interoperability rather than the over-all integration of the two annotation schemes, especially concerning spatial, temporal, and spatio-temporal measure expressions. We claim that only a few minor modifications need to be made to resolve any formal, but not necessarily terminological or semantic inconsistencies between the standards in annotating measure expressions, either spatial or temporal, while keeping their original overall annotation schemes almost intact.

The rest of the paper develops as follows: Section 2 Review of ISO-TimeML and ISOspace, Section 3 Formal Inconsistencies, Section 4 Partial Merging, Section 5 Informal Semantics, and Section 6 Concluding Remarks.

2 Review of ISO-TimeML and ISOspace

In this section we briefly introduce ISO-TimeML (ISO, 2012b) and ISOspace (ISO, 2014a) that specify how to annotate measure expressions, temporal and spatial, respectively. For illustrations, we focus on the two basic entity types of measure: duration and distance.

2.1 Overview: Duration and Distance

Duration and distance are two types of a basic entity, named *measure*, that share structurally common features. As measure expressions, they are both structured as a pair `<n,u>`, consisting of a numeric standing for quantity and a unit, possibly with a modifier that is optional: e.g., (1) *three*$_n$ *days*$_u$ and (2) *nearly*$_{mod}$ *130*$_n$ *km*$_u$.

Furthermore, they are also interpreted at times as involving a temporal or a spatial interval, delimited by two end points, as shown below:

(2) a. *We drove [*$_{endPoint1}$ *three days* $_{endPoint2}$*] before [Christmas Day]*$_{t2=endPoint2}$.

b. *We barely drove [*$_{endPoint1}$ *50km* $_{endPoint2}$*] from [Pearson Airport]*$_{pl1=endPoint1}$.

Here (a) is interpreted as an event of driving that occurred on December 22 (`endPoint1`). Similarly, (b) is interpreted as a motion of driving with an event path which covered the distance of 50 kilometers (`endPoint2`).[7] In the ensuing two subsections 2.2 and 2.3, we illustrate how durations and distances are annotated by ISO-TimeML and ISOspace, respectively, and represented in XML.

2.2 Durations in ISO-TimeML

There are two sorts of temporal expressions in our dataset (1) that are both treated by ISO-TimeML as durations:[8]

(3) a. *We had to drive for* **more than 6 hours**$_{t1}$.

```
<TIMEX3 xml:id="t1" type="DURATION" value="P6H" mod="moreThan"/>
```

[6]See also Bunt (2015) in this volume for the main ideas of ISO SemAF Principles.

[7]This event is a directed and terminated dynamic motion each movement of which can be described structurally as a pair $<l_i, t_j>$ consisting of a location l_i and an associated time t_j that increases incrementally. It thus forms an event path which is again analyzed as a sequence of movements with at least two end points, initial and terminal: $<l_0, t_i>, <l_1, t_{i+1}>, \ldots, <l_m, t_n>$. Here, the distance of an event path is measured as a length between each pair of a location and a time in the sequence. See (Mani and Pustejovsky, 2012), pp. 90-107, for further details on directed motion and dynamic interval temporal logic (DITL).

[8]For the sake of illustrations, dataset fragments are inline annotated with their IDs in this paper, while the specification of the attribute @target or @markable is ommitted from the annotation of basic entities in ISO-TimeML or ISOspace, respectively.

b. *We drove to Niagara Falls* $[_{t21}$**three days**$_{t22}]_{t2}$ *before* **Christmas Day**$_{t3}$.

```
<TIMEX3 xml:id="t2" type="DURATION" value="P3D"
beginPoint="#t21" endPoint="#t22"/>
<TIMEX3 xml:id="t3" type="DATE" value="XXXX-12-25"/>
<TIMEX3 xml:id="t21" target="" type="DATE" value="XXXX-12-22"
temporalFunction="TRUE" anchorTimeID="#t3"/>
```
[9]

Both of the temporal expressions [*more than 6 hours*]$_{t1}$ and [*three days*]$_{t2}$ are measure expressions, each specified with a numeric (quantity) and a unit. They carry different sorts of information, however. The first expression `t1` refers to an amount of time, the amount of time consumed by the motion of driving. On the other hand, the latter expression `t2` refers to a time interval that identifies Christmas (`t3=XXXX-12-25`) with its end point `t22` and another date (`XXXX-12-22`) with its beginning point `t21`.

Then there are two different link relations in ISO-TimeML: (1) <MLINK> between the event$_{e1}$ of driving and the amount of time `t1` and (2) <TLINK> between that same event$_{e1}$ and the initial point of time `t21` of a time interval `t2`, as shown below:

(4) a. *We had to drive*$_{e1}$ *for* [**more than 6 hours**]$_{t1}$.

```
<MLINK eventID="#e1" relatedToTime="#t1" relType="MEASURES"/>
```

b. *We drove*$_{e1}$ *to Niagara Falls* $[_{t21}$**three days**$]_{t2}$ *before Christmas Day.*

```
<TLINK eventID="#e1" relatedToTime="#t21" relType="DURING"/>
```

Here the event (motion) of driving$_{e1}$ in Example (a) is linked to the amount of time$_{t1}$ that it consumed, while that same event$_{e1}$ in Example (b) is anchored to the date$_{t21}$ (December 22) during which it occurred.

2.3 Distances in ISOspace

There are three quantitatively explicit spatial measure expressions in our dataset Travel Log (1):

(5) a. *Niagara Falls is approximately 130km (80 miles) southwest of Toronto.*

b. *Niagara is about 123km (76 miles) from Pearson Airport.*

c. *We stopped for coffee after barely driving 50km (a little over 30 miles) from Pearson Airport.*

According to ISOspace, these measure expressions are annotated as below:

(6) a.
```
<measure xml:id="mes1" markable="approximately 130km"
value="130" unit="km" mod="approx"/>
```

b.
```
<measure xml:id="mes2" markable="about 123km"
value="123" unit="km" mod="approx"/>
```

c.
```
<measure xml:id="mes3" markable="barely ...50km"
value="50" unit="km" mod="equalOrLess"/>
```

While the annotation of these basic entities (measures) is routine, their linking relations slightly differ from one another:

(7) a. [*Niagara Falls*]$_{pl1}$ *is* [**approximately 130km**]$_{mes1}$ *southwest*$_{ss1}$ *of Toronto*$_{pl2}$

```
<oLink xml:id="ol1" figure="#pl1" ground="#pl2" trigger="#ss1"
relType="southwest" frameType="absolute" referencePt="southwest"
projective="true"/>
<mLink xml:id="ml1" relType="distance" figure="#pl1" ground="#pl2"
trigger="#mes1" val="#mes1"/>
```

b. *Niagara*$_{pl1}$ *is* [**about 123km**]$_{mes2}$ *from*$_{ss2}$ [*Pearson Airport*]$_{pl3}$.

```
<mLink xml:id="ml2" relType="distance" figure="#pl1"
ground="#pl3" trigger="#mes2" val="#mes2"/>
```

[9] `<TIMEX3 xml:id="t21"/>` may be treated as an element, called *non-consuming tag*, which has no associated markable expression in text, thus the value of its attribute `@target` being empty `""`. See ISOspace (ISO, 2014a), A.3.4 Special Section: Non-consuming tags.

c. *We stopped for coffee after* **barely**$_{mes3}$ *driving*$_{m1}$ *[***50km***]*$_{mes3}$.

```
<mLink xml:id="ml3" relType="generalDimension" figure="#m1"
ground="#m1" trigger="#mes3" val="#mes3"/>
```

Examples (a) and (b) both represent a `distance` type relation, while Example (a) carries additional information about the orientation expressed by the spatial signal *southwest*. On the other hand, example (c) is annotated as referring to a `general dimension` type relation in ISOspace,[10] but may also be annotated as referring to a relation of the `distance` type grounded to the event-path created by the motion *drive*, as will be discussed in the following Section 3.

3 Formal Inconsistencies

The specification of semantic annotation schemes can be inconsistent in three different ways. The first two are introduced as *terminological* and *semantic* inconsistencies in ISO SemAF Principles[11] to be briefly discussed in the following Subsection 3.1. The third kind of inconsistency that we name *formal inconsistency* is discussed in Subsection 3.2.

3.1 Terminologial or Semantic Inconsistency

Terminological inconsistency arises if two different terms are used for one and the same concept. For example, ISOspace has an element named *measure* for the concept referring to a quantity, whereas ISO SemAF Principles (ISO, 2014c) proposes the name *amount* for the same concept. Hence, the use of these two terms (names) is terminologically inconsistent.

Semantic inconsistency is caused by the use of a term for two different concepts. In ISO-TimeML, the term *event* refers to an eventuality, whereas it refers to a non-motion event in ISOspace. Hence, the use of the term *event* in ISOspace is semantically inconsistent with its use in ISO-TimeML. The term *duration* in ISO-TimeML refers to an amount of time and also to an interval of time. The use of this term is again semantically inconsistent.

The use of the tag (name of an element) `<event>` can, however, be intrinsically consistent within ISOspace, for it explicitly specifies the tag `<event>` as standing for a non-motion event (e.g., love), while using the tag `<motion>` to annotate motion verbs such as *drive* or *run*. The use of the tag `<event>` in ISOspace becomes inconsistent only if ISOspace is integrated with ISO-TimeML to form a single annotation scheme, for the tag `<event>` in ISO-TimeML stands for eventuality.

3.2 Formal Inconsistency between or within Standards

3.2.1 Intrinsic vs Extrinsic Inconsistency

The term *formal inconsistency* is here used to refer to structural differences between or within standards in their specification of annotation schemes. Each annotation scheme has two levels of specification: one is the level of specification, called *abstract syntax*, and the other the level, called *concrete syntax*, (e.g., an XML serialization of an abstract syntax for temporal annotation). The concrete syntax of an annotation scheme specifies how to represent the annotations specified by the abstract syntax. Formal inconsistency may occur between an abstract syntax and its associated concrete syntax when the concrete syntax fails to properly represent the annotations based on the abstract syntax.[12] Such a case of formal inconsistency, as is described now, we call *intrinsic* inconsistency.

In contrast, there is another case of formal inconsistency which we call *extrinsic* inconsistency. Given at least a pair of markables which are of two different sorts, but which have isomorphic (similar) structures (e.g., *We drove for nearly 2 hours.* vs. *We drove nearly 50 miles*), two annotation schemes are understood to be formally inconsistent, if and only if, they specify different sets of basic entities or link relations over them or associate different lists of attributes and possible values for some of the entities or links.

If an annotation scheme is intrinsically inconsistent, then it is a serious problem for the annotation scheme itself. A concrete syntax becomes useless. Extrinsic inconsistency causes no problem for the interoperability of two annotation schemes, unless they are merged into a single annotation scheme. In the rest of Subsection 3.2, we focus on possible cases of formal inconsistency between the two standards, ISO-TimeML and ISOspace, in the annotation of measure expressions (distances vs durations) that are considered isomorphic in Subsubsection

[10]See ISOspace (ISO, 2014a), A.6.5.2, Example (c)

[11]See ISO DIS 24617-6 SemAF Principles ISO (2014c), Clause 9.3 Quantities and measures, pp. 18-19.

[12]See Ide and Romary (2004), ISO 24612 LAF (ISO, 2012a), Bunt (2010), Bunt (2011), and Bunt and Pustejovsky (2010) for the distinction between annotation and its representation, and also between an abstract syntax and a concrete syntax.

3.2.2 and their annotation of links that relate and other basic entities to measure in Subsubsection 3.2.3. We finally discuss the formal inconsistency of specifying optional attributes in ISOspace and ISO-TimeML in Subsubsection 3.2.4.

3.2.2 Annotation of Measure Expressions

As mentioned in Subclause 2.1, measure expressions are treated in abstract terms as consisting of a pair <n,u>, where n is a numeric referring to some quantity and u a unit. The measure expressions *nearly 2 hours* and *about 123 km* are similar in structure. In representing their annotations, ISO-TimeML ad ISOspace are different from each other or extrinsically inconsistent (to use our term), as shown in Example (8):

(8) a. *nearly 2 hours*
ISO-TimeML: `<TIMEX3 xml:id="t1" type="DURATION" value="P2H" mod="APPROX"/>`

b. *about 123 km*
ISOspace: `<measure xml:id="mes1" value="123" unit="km" mod="approx"/>`

First, the tags of the two elements are different: <TIMEX3> vs <measure>. Second, ISO-TimeML specifies the type "DURATION" of its element <TIMEX3>, while ISOspace specifies no type for its element <measure>. Third, the value for the measure is represented as one chunk "P2H" in ISO-TimeML, while ISOspace represents the value of a measure separately from its unit by introducing two attributes @value and @unit.

In specifying ways of assigning a value (e.g., P6H) to the attribute @value for temporal expressions, ISO-TimeML follows ISO 8601 (ISO, 2004). The value P6H stands for "a period (P) of 6 hours (H)" and the period (P) is understood to be a duration of time or an amount of time, thus allowing a proper interpretation of the value P6H as a duration. As is argued in ISO SemAF Principles, the specification of annotating amounts of time (e.g., *nearly two hours*) in ISO-TimeML is, however, intrinsically inconsistent, for the attribute-value specification value="P6H", for one thing, fails to conform to the abstract specification of annotating measure expressions.

Unlike ISO-TimeML, ISOspace is found intrinsically consistent. Consider the following list of attributes and possible values for the element, tagged <measure>, in XML:

(9) Attributes of <measure>[13]
attributes = identifier, markable, value, [unit], [mod], [comment];
value = "real" | CDATA;
unit = CDATA;
mod = CDATA;

Bracketed attributes are optional ones, while non-bracketed ones are required attributes. There are two alternative values for the attribute @value: either a real number with its unit specified or any CDATA such as far with no unit specified. To allow non-explicit measure expressions as markables, ISOspace treats the attribute @unit as an optional (implied) attribute.

Here are two illustrations, one for an explicit measure expression and another for a non-explicit measure expression:

(10) a. `<measure xml:id="mes1" markable="about 123 kilometers" value="123" unit="km" mod="approx"/>`

b. `<measure xml:id="mes2" markable="very far" value="far" mod="very"/>`[14]

Hence, the concrete representation in XML of annotations of measure expressions in ISOspace is shown to be intrinsically consistent with some of its abstract specifications or the abstract syntax in general.

ISOspace may be extended to annotate temporal durations simply by adding temporal units to the list of possible values of the attribute @unit. Here is an illustration:

(11) a. *more than 6 hours*

b. `<measure xml:id="mes1" markable="more than 6 hours" value="6" unit="hour" mod="moreThan"/>`

[13]The format of listing these attributes follows the representation language of ISO/IEC (1996)'s Extended BNF.

[14]The adjectival or adverbial intensifier *very* is here treated as a value of @mod. It is not explicitly listed among the possible values of @mod, but is allowed by CDATA.

ISO DIS 24617-6 SemAF Principles argues against the representation of quantity modifiers as attribute-value pairs (e.g., `mod="moreThan"`) of the element `<measure>`. Instead, it proposes that a quantity modifier should be treated as a relation between two amounts or measurements, as shown below:[15]

(12) *We had to drive for more than 6 hours*

```
<amount xml:id="a1" target="#range(token6,token9)>
<amount xml:id="a2" target="#token8,#token9" num="6" unit="hour"/>
<relation xml:id="r1" arg1="#a1" arg2="#a2" relType="greaterThan"/>
```

This representation of a quantity modification should be formally and intrinsically *consistent* with the abstract syntax that specifies the notion of a quantity modification.

3.2.3 Measure Links

ISOspace introduces the tag `<mLink>` to annotate and represent the linking of events (motions) or any other relevant entities to a measure such as a distance or other spatial dimensions. Here is an example:

(13) a. *We drove*$_{m1}$ *[about 122 kilometers]*$_{mes1}$.

b.
```
<motion xml:id="m1" motionType="manner"/>
<measure xml:id="mes1" value="122" unit="km" mod="approx"/>
<mLink xml:id="ml1" relType="distance" figure="#m1" ground="#m1"
trigger="#mes1" val="#mes1"/>
```

This representation is based on the following specification of ISOspace:

(14) Current List of Attributes for the Element `<mLink>`[16]
attributes = `identifier, markable, [trigger], [figure], [ground], relType, val, [endPoint1], [endPoint2], [comment];`

This specification fails to be consistent with the abstract structure `<e1,e2,R>` of a link `R` that relates a basic entity `e1` to another basic entity `e2`, for there is no pair of required attributes in the current list (14) of attributes for the element `<mLink>` which refer to two related entities.[17] Links are basically binary relations between two entities. All of the links, `<TLINK>`, `<ALINK>`, `<SLINK>` and `<MLINK>`, in ISO-TimeML (ISO, 2012b) are binary relations between two entities, each having a pair of required attributes that specify a pair of entities that are to be related. `<TLINK>`, for instance, relates an event to a time or another event, thus having two required attributes like `@eventID` and `relatedToTimeID` or `relatedToEventID` also with a third required attribute `@relType` specifying the type of their relation.

This problem can, however, be easily fixed by treating the attributes `@figure` and `ground` as well as the attribute `relType` in the list (14) as required attributes and then making the two attributes `@figure` and `ground` stand for the two basic entities `e1` and `e2` that are to be linked by the relation `R` specified by the required attribute `relType`. The attribute `@val` is no longer necessary, for it is replaced by the newly required attribute `ground` which is now understood as referring to the value of an element `<measure>`.

(15) Modified List of Attributes for the Element `<mLink>`
attributes = `identifier, markable, figure, ground, relType, [trigger], [endPoint1], [endPoint2], [comment];`

With this modified specification (15), the measure link, tagged as `<mLink>`, in ISOspace is now understood as a binary relation from a motion, a location or some other spatial entity (`figure`) to a measure (`ground`), as shown below:

(16) a. *We drove*$_{m1}$ *[about 122 kilometers]*$_{mes1}$.

b. Old:
```
<mLink xml:id="ml1" relType="distance" figure="#m1"
ground="#m1" trigger="#mes1" val="#mes1"/>
```

[15] See SemAF Principles (ISO, 2014c), Clause 9.3 Quantifiers and measures, pp. 18-19, example (16).

[16] List A.13 in ISOspace (ISO, 2014a).

[17] The specification of `<oLink>` and `<moveLink>` also run into the same problem and should be the topic for discussion on another occasion.

c. New:
```
<mLink xml:id="ml1" relType="distance" figure="#m1"
ground="#mes1"/>
```

Now the two measure links in ISOspace and ISO-TimeML structurally resemble each other, as shown below:

(17) a. *We had to drive*$_{e1/m1}$ *[about 122 kilometers]*$_{mes1}$ *for [more than 6 hours]*$_{t1}$.

b. ISOspace
```
<mLink relType="distance" figure="#m1" ground="#mes1"/>
```

c. ISO-TimeML
```
<MLINK relType="MEASURES" eventID="#e1" relatedToTime="#t1">
```

These two are formally consistent, although they are terminologically inconsistent.

Compare now this modified treatment of the measure link (`<mLink>`) in ISOspace with the proposal of ISO SemAF Principles (ISO, 2014c) that the measure link both in ISO-TimeML and ISOspace be replaced by `<srLink>` for semantic roles, introduced by SemAF-SR (ISO, 2014b). Here is an example:

(18) a. *I would walk*$_{m1/ev1}$ *[500 miles]*$_{mes1/am1}$.

b. ISOspace:
```
<measure xml:id="mes1" value="500" unit="mile"/>
<mLink xml:id="ml1" figure="#m1" ground="#mes1" relType="distance"/>
```

c. SemAF Principles/SemAF-SR:
```
<timeAmount xml:id="am1" aNum="500" unit="mile"/>
<srLink xml:id="sr1" arg1="#ev1" arg2="#am1" semRole="distance"/>
```

These two treatments are formally consistent, for they both conform to the abstract structure `<e1,e2,R>` of the binary link relation.

3.2.4 Specification of Optional Attributes

In ISO TimeML, the annotation of information related to an interval with its `@beginPoint` and `@endPoint` is associated with the basic entity element `<TIMEX3 type="DURATION"/>`. In ISOspace, on the other hand, the annotation of information related to a path with its `@endPoint1` and `@endPoint2` is associated with the link `<mLink>`. Here are examples:

(19) a. ISOspace:[18]

The width of the office$_{pl3}$ *is [25 feet]*$_{mes5}$ *from the bookcase*$_{se3}$ *to the [white board]*$_{se4}$.
```
<measue xml:id="mes5" value="25" unit="ft"/>
<mLink xml:id="ml5" relType="distance" figure="#pl3" ground="#mes5"
endPoint1="#se3" endPoint2="#se4"/>
```

b. ISO-TimeML:[19]

We left$_{e6}$ *[*$_{t61}$ *two weeks* $_{t62}$*]*$_{t6}$ *from [June 7, 2003]*$_{t7}$
```
<EVENT xml:id="e6" pred="LEAVE" tense="PAST"/>
<TIMEX3 xml:id="t6" type="DURATION" value="P2W"
beginPoint="#t61" endPoint="#t62"/>
<TIMEX3 xml:id="t7" type="DATE" value="2003-06-07"/>
<TIMEX3 xml:id="t62" type="DATE" value="2003-06-21"
temporalFunction="true" anchorTimeID="#t7"/>
<TLINK eventID="e1" relatedToTime="#t62" relType="DURING"/>
```

ISO SemAF Principles freely allows the specification of optional attributes associated with basic entities or links. Hence, the variation shown above may not be considered as causing formal inconsistency. Nevertheless, they create a problem for the integration of ISO-TimeML and ISOspace for the annotation of measure expressions and their links, as will be discussed in Section 4.

[18]Taken from ISOspace (ISO, 2014a), Annex A.6.5.2 Example (d), p.48, with some modifications.

[19]Taken from ISO-TimeML (ISO, 2012b), Clause 7.3.4.2 `<TIMEX3>`, page 17, Example (13) with the addition of `<TLINK>`.

4 Partial Merging

Two annotation schemes are interoperable only if each of them is formally and intrinsically consistent. They can also refer to each other, as shown below:

(20) a. *We had to drive*$_{m1}$ *[about 123km]*$_{mes1}$ *for [more than 6 hours]*$_{t1}$.

b.
```
<semAF xml:id="sem01">
<isoSpace xml:id="sAnn01">
<motion xml:id="m1" type="drive"/>
<measure xml:id="mes1" value="123" unit="km" mod="approx"/>
<mLink xml:id="ml1" figure="#m1" ground="#mes1" relType="distance"/>
</isoSpace>
<isoTimeML xml:id="tAnn01">
<TIMEX3 xml:id="t1" type="DURATION" value="P6H" mod="moreThan"/>
<MLINK eventID="#m1" relatedToTime="#t1" relType="MEASURES"/>
</isoTimeML>
</semAF>
```

Here, `<isoSpace>` shows how the spatial measure (distance) expression `mes1` is annotated, while `<isoTimeML>` shows the annotation of the temporal measure (duration) expression `t1`. Furthermore, `<isoTimeML>` allows its `<MLINK>` to refer to the element `<motion xml:id="m1"/>` in `<isoSpace>` for the value `#m1` of the attribute `@eventID`. Otherwise, the motion of *drive*$_{m1}$ may not be understood as referring to one and the same event of driving.

Despite their intrinsic formal consistency, these two annotation schemes are extrinsically inconsistent. This inconsistency can easily be resolved by introducing a few modifications into ISOspace and then by merging the treatment of temporal measure expressions into it. To merge the annotation of temporal measure expressions such as *more than 6 hours* into ISOspace, as in Illustration (21), it is only necessary to extend the list of possible values for the attribute `@unit` for the element `measure` of ISOspace to include temporal units such as `hours`. This is done automatically because that list is an open list, consisting of any `CDATA`.

(21)
```
<isoSpace xml:id="sAnn01">
<motion xml:id="m1" markable="#token4" type="drive"/>
<measure xml:id="mes1" value="123" unit="km" mod="approx"/>
<measure xml:id="mes2" value=6" unit="hours" mod="moreThan"/>
<mLink xml:id="ml1" figure="#m1" ground="#mes1" relType="distance"/>
<mLink xml:id="ml1" figure="#m1" ground="#mes2" relType="duration"/>
</isoSpace>
```

Here, the list of values for the attribute `@relType` of the element `<mLink>` is also extended to `"duration"`.[20]

Such merging, however, requires further modifications. Consider the following pair of examples:

(22) a. *We left*$_{e1}$ *[*$_{t11}$ *two weeks* $_{t12}$*]*$_{t1}$ *from*$_{s1}$ *[June 7, 2003]*$_{t2}$.

b. *We drove*$_{m1}$ *[about 123 km]*$_{mes1}$ *from*$_{ms1}$ *[Pearson Airport]*$_{pl1}$.

These two sentences are syntactically the same except that (a) contains two temporal expressions, a duration (`t1`) and a date (`t2`), while (b) contains two spatial expressions, a distance measure (`mes1`) and a location (`pl1`). Their annotations are thus expected to be structurally the same, but the current versions of the two annotation schemes, ISO-TimeML and ISOspace, however, present two different annotation structures.

(23) a. ISO-TimeML
```
<EVENT xml:id="e1" pred="LEAVE" tense="past"/>
<TIMEX3 xml:id="t1" type="DURATION" value="P2W"
beingPoint="#t11" endPoint="#t12"/>
<SIGNAL xml:id="s1" pred="FROM"/>
<TIMEX3 xml:id="t2" type="date" value="2003-06-07"/>
<TIMEX3 xml:id="t12" target="" type="date" value="2003-06-21"
temporalFunction="true" anchorTimeID="#t2"/>
<TLINK eventID="#e1" relatedToTime="#t12" relType="DURING"/>
```

[20]Later, this value will be changed to `"runtime"`.

b. ISOspace

```
<motion xml:id="m1" type="drive" tense="past"/>
<measure xml:id="mes1" value="123" unit="km" mod="approx"/>
<signal xml:id="ms1" markable="from"/>
<mLink xml:id="ml1" relType="distance" figure="#m1"
ground="#m1" val="#mes1" endPoint1="#pl1" />
```

There are at least three possible ways to integrate ISO-TimeML and ISOspace for the annotation of measure expressions. One way is to modify the part of ISO-TimeML which annotates durations and merge it into ISOspace, as was shown in Example (21), another way is to take the opposite approach, and a third way to follow ISO SemAF Principles[21] and merge the two different annotation schemes of measure expressions, both spatial and temporal, into a new annotation scheme or ISO SemAF-SR (semantic roles) (ISO, 2014b). For now, we take the first approach and show how ISO-TimeML's annotation (23a) can be partially merged into ISOspace by extending the current version of ISOspace to accommodate parts of ISO-TimeML. Here is an illustration:

(24) a. *We drove$_{m1}$ to Niagara Falls [$_{t1}$ three days $_{t2}$]$_{mes1}$ before$_{s1}$ [Christmas Day]$_{t3}$.*

b.

```
<semAF xml:id="sem02">
<isoSpace xml:id="sAnn02">
<motion xml:id="m1" type="drive" tense="past"/>
<measure xml:id="mes1" value="3" unit="day"/>
<mLink xml:id="ml1" figure="#t1" ground="#mes1"
relType="beginPointOf"/>
</isoSpace>
<isoTimeML xml:id="tAnn02>
<TIMEX3 xml:id="t1" target="" type="date" value="XXXX-12-22"
temporalFunction="true" anchorTimeID="#t3" mLinkID="#ml1"/>
<SIGNAL xml:id="s1" pred="BEFORE"/>
<TIMEX3 xml:id="t3" type="DATE" value="XXXX-12-25"/>
<TLINK xml:id="tl1" timeID="#mes1" relatedToTime="#t3"
relType="BEFORE"/>
<TLINK xml:id="tl2" eventID="#m1" relatedToTime="#t1"
relType="DURING"/>
</isoTimeML>
</semAF>
```

Here, the link `<mLink xml:id="ml1">` is interpreted as stating that the date `t1` is the initial point of the time interval with its length being "three days" `mes1`. The calculation of the date (`date(t1)=XXXX-12-22`) is then triggered by `mLinkID="#ml1"` with its interval value `mes1=[3,day]` and also anchored to the date `date(t3)=XXXX-12-25` of `anchorTimeID="#t3"` in `<isoTimeML>`.

5 Informal Semantics

For the semantic justification of the proposed annotations of measure expressions, we show in this section how some of them are interpreted. Consider the following dataset segments, taken from Travel Log (1):[22]

(25) Semi-annotated Dataset 2
We$_{se1}$ ... drove$_{m1}$ from [Pearson Airport]$_{pl0}$ to [Niagara Falls]$_{pl1}$ [$_{t11}$three days$_{t12}$]$_{t1}$ before [Christmas Day]$_{t2}$. We$_{se1}$ drove$_{m1}$ to$_{ms1}$ Niagara$_{pl1}$ [about 122 kilometers]$_{mes1}$ for$_{s}$ [more than 6 hours]$_{mes2}$ at [an average speed of 20 kilometers per hour]$_{mes3}$.

5.1 Interpreting Event Paths

Here we may or may not introduce a non-consuming tag $\emptyset_{p1}$ for an event path from [Pearson Airport]$_{pl0}$ to Niagara$_{pl1}$. The following are two versions of an expected logical form for Dataset 2, one for a case with no event path annotated and another for a case with an event path annotated:

[21] See SemAF Principles, Clause 8.2 Spatial and temporal relations as semantic roles, and other places.

[22] For simplicity's sake, the same IDs are assigned to coreferential expressions in this dataset.

(26) a. No event path annotated:
$[drive(m_1) \wedge agent(se_1, m_1) \wedge goal(pl_1, m_1) \wedge distance(m_1) \approx [122, km] \wedge runtime(m_1) \geq [6, hour] \wedge speed(m_1) =_{average} [20, km/h]]$

b. An event path annotated:
$[drive(m_1) \wedge agent(se_1, m_1) \wedge goal(pl_1, m_1) \wedge path(p_1, m_1, pl_0, pl_1) \wedge distance(p_1) \approx [122, km] \wedge runtime(m_1) \geq [6, hour] \wedge speed(m_1) =_{average} [20, km/h]]$

In (a), $distance(m_1)$ is interpreted as the quantity (length) of a distance traversed by the motion of driving (m_1). In (b), on the other hand, $distance(p_1)$ is interpreted as the quantity (length) of a path traversed by the motion of driving (m_1) from Pearson Airport (pl_0) to Niagara (pl_1). The second interpretation is more detailed than the first one, but they are practically equivalent and equally acceptable interpretations.

Here we simply focus on the parts of the interpretations that are related to measures. Consider:

(27) $[drive(m_1) \wedge distance(m_1) \approx [122, km]]$

This is based on the following annotation:

(28)
```
<motion xml:id="m1" type="drive" motionType="path"/>
<measure xml:id="mes1" value="122" unit="km" mod="approx"/>
<mLink xml:id="ml1" figure="#m1" ground="#mes1" relType="distance"/>
```

Then we have:

(29) Interpetation 1:
(i) $\sigma(m_1) := drive(m_1)$
(ii) $\sigma(mes_1) := q_{measured}(mes_1) \approx [122, km]$
(iii) $\sigma(ml_1) := q_{distance}(m_1) = q_{measured}(mes_1)$
(iv) $\sigma(s_1) := [drive(m_1) \wedge q_{distance}(m_1) \approx [122, km]]$

Here $q_{measured}(mes_1)$ is a quantity measured at a particular situation mes_1, while $q_{distance}(m_1)$ is interpreted as the quantity (length) of a distance traversed by a motion m_1.

We can also have:

(30) Interpretation 2:
(i) $\sigma(m_1) := drive(m_1)$
(ii) $\sigma(p_1) := path(p_1, m_1, pl_0, pl_1)$
(iii) $\sigma(mes_1) := q_{measured}(mes_1) \approx [122, km]$
(iv) $\sigma(ml_1) := q_{distance}(p_1) = q_{measured}(mes_1)$
(v) $\sigma(s_1) := [drive(m_1) \wedge q_{distance}(p_1) \approx [122, km]]$

This is the interpretation when a path is introduced as a non-consuming tag into the annotation.

5.2 Interpreting Amount of Time

Here is another illustration:

(31) a. Fragment1: *[We drove*$_{m1}$ *for*$_{ts1}$ *[more than 6 hours]*$_{mes2}$*.]*$_{s2}$

b. Annotation:
```
<motion xml:id="m1" type="drive" motionType="manner"/>
<measure xml:id="mes2" value="6" unit="hour" mod="moreThan"/>
<mLink xml:id="ml2" relType="runtime" figure="#m1" ground="#mes2"
trigger="#ts1"/>
```

c. Interpretation:
(i) $\sigma(m_1) := drive(m_1)$
(ii) $\sigma(mes_2) := q_{measured}(mes_2) \geq [6, hour]$
(iii) $\sigma(ml_2) := q_{runtime}(m_1) = q_{measured}(mes_2)$
(iv) $\sigma(s_2) := [drive(m_1) \wedge q_{runtime}(m_1) \geq [6, hour]]$

5.3 Interpreting Intervals

The measure expression *three days* may be used with a date expression *Christmas Day* as in the following dataset fragment (32). The annotation of this fragment has been presented in Section 4, Example (24). Here the measure expression is understood as providing information on either the initial or the terminal boundary of an interval of time with its quantity measured to be the length of three days.

(32) a. Fragment2: *[We ... drove$_{m1}$ ... [$_{t1}$three days]$_{mes1}$ before [Christmas Day]$_{t2}$.]$_{sem02}$*

b. Annotation: based on Example (24).

c. Interpretation:
(i) $\sigma(m_1) := drive(m_1)$
(ii) $\sigma(mes_1) := q_{measured}(mes_1) = [3, day]$
(iii) $\sigma(ml_1) := begins(t_1, \iota(mes_1)) \wedge length(\iota(mes_1)) = [3, day]$
(iv) $\sigma(t_1) := [month(12, t_2) \wedge day(22, t_2)]$
(v) $\sigma(tl_1) := before(\iota(mes1), t_2)$
(vi) $\sigma(t_3) := [month(12, t_2) \wedge day(25, t_2)]$
(vii) $\sigma(tl_2) := [drive(m_1) \wedge during(m_1, t_1)]$
(viii) $\sigma(sem_{02}) := [drive(m_1) \wedge begins(t_1, \iota(mes_1)) \wedge length(\iota(mes_1)) = [3, day] \wedge month(12, t_1) \wedge day(22, t_1) \wedge during(m_1, t_1) \wedge before(\iota(mes_1), t_2) \wedge month(12, t_2) \wedge day(25, t_2)]$

The function ι maps an amount of time to an interval with its length measured to be that amount.

6 Concluding Remarks

This paper has reviewed some cases of formal inconsistency between the two recently published ISO standards, ISO 24617-1 ISO-TimeML (ISO, 2012b) and ISO 24617-7 ISOspace (ISO, 2014a) in annotating measure expressions, temporal and spatial, respectively. With a focus on durations (amounts of time) and distances, it has shown how the part of ISO-TimeML that annotates durations can be merged into ISOspace but with some modifications to resolve formal inconsistencies between the two standards. Following ISO 24617-6 SemAF Principles (ISO, 2014c) and Bunt (2015), it has also briefly examined the possibility of further generalizing the annotation scheme for measure expressions or incorporating it into `<srLink>` of ISO (2014b), but left it as an open issue. Sometimes a domain-specific modular approach with some overlaps licensed and tasks distributed can be considered of more practical use with greater efficiency than a single unified and theoretically compact treatment. The ubiquity of measure expressions in language and their use over various domains may also require a separate annotation scheme that can generally apply to various parts of semantic annotation. This paper has done its best not to propose extensive revisions, but attempted to resolve any formal inconsistencies with minimal modifications.

Acknowledgements

I owe thanks to David Lovisek for modifying the travel log, to Harry Bunt, Suk-Jin Chang, Jae-woong Choe, Thierry Declerck, Koiti Hasida, James Pustejovsky, and other reviewers for their constructive comments, and especially to Roland Hausser who helped produce the final version.

References

Branimir, B., J. Castaño, R. Gaizauskas, B. Ingria, G. Katz, B. Knippen, J. Littman, I. Mani, J. Pustejovsky, A. Sanfilippo, A. See, A. Setzer, R. Saurí, A. Stubbs, B. Sundheim, S. Symonenko, and M. Verhagen (2005). *TimeML 1.2.1: A Formal Specification Language for Events and Temporal Expressions.*

Bunt, H. (2010). A methodology for designing semantic annotation languages exploring semantic- syntactic isomorphisms. In A. Fang, N. Ide, and J. Webster (Eds.), *Proceedings of the Second International Conference on Global Interoperability for Language Resources (ICGL 2010)*, Hong Kong, pp. 29–46. Department of Chinese, Translation and Linguistics, City Univesity of Hong Kong.

Bunt, H. (2011). Introducing abstract syntaxt + semantics in semantic annotation, and its consequences for the annotation of time and events. In E. Lee and A. Yoon (Eds.), *Recent Trends in Language and Knowledge Processing*, Seoul, pp. 157–204. Hankookmunhwasa.

Bunt, H. (2015). On the principles of interoperable semantic annotation. In H. Bunt (Ed.), *Proceedings of the Eleventh Joint ISO-ACL/SIGSEM Workshop on Interoperable Semantic Annotation (ISA-11)*, Queen Mary University of London, pp. xx–yy. A satellite workshop of IWCS 2015.

Bunt, H. and J. Pustejovsky (2010). Annotating temporal and event quantification. In H. Bunt (Ed.), *Proceedings of the Fifth Joint ISO-ACL/SIGSEM Workshop on Interoperable Semantic Annotation (ISA-5)*, Hong Kong, pp. 15–22. Department of Chinese, Translation and Linguistics, City University of Hong Kong.

Ide, N. and L. Romary (2004). International standard for a linguistic annotation framework. *Natural Language Engineering*, 10, 211225.

ISO (2004). *ISO 8601:2004 Data elements and interchange formats – Information interchange – Representation of dates and times*. Geneva: ISO.

ISO (2012a). *ISO 24612:2012 Language resource management - Linguistic annotation framework (LAF)*. Geneva: ISO. ISO Working Group:TC 37/SC 4/WG 1, Convenor and Project leader: Nancy Ide.

ISO (2012b). *ISO 24617-1:2012 Language resource management - Semantic annotation framework - Part 1: Time and events (SemAF-Time, ISO-TimeML)*. Geneva: ISO. ISO Working Group:TC 37/SC 4/WG 2, Editors: James Pustejvosky (chair), Harry Bunt, Kiyong Lee (convenor and project leader), Bran Boguraev, and Nancy Ide in cooperation with the TimeML Working Group, http://www.timeml.org.

ISO (2014a). *ISO 24617-7:2014 Language resource management - Part 7: Spatial information (ISOspace)*. Geneva: ISO. ISO Working Group: TC 37/SC 4/WG 2, Project leaders: James Pustejovsky and Kiyong Lee, supported by the ISOspace Working Group headed by James Pustejvosky at Brandeis University, Waltham, MA, U.S.A. The following is the homepage for the ISO-Space project <https://sites.google.com/site/wikiisospace/>.

ISO (2014b). *ISO 24617-7:2014 Language resource management - Semantic annotation framework - Part 4: Semantic roles (SemAF-SR)*. Geneva: ISO. ISO Working Group: TC 37/SC 4/WG 2, Project leader: Martha Palmer.

ISO (2014c). *ISO DIS 24617-6 Language resource management - Semantic annotation framework - Part 6: Basic principles (SemAF-Basics)*. Geneva: ISO. ISO Working Group: TC 37/SC 4/WG 2, Project leader: Harry Bunt.

ISO/IEC (1996). *ISO/IEC 14977:1996(E), Information technology – Syntactic metalanguage – Extended BNF.* Geneva: ISO.

Lee, K. (2012). Interoperable spatial and temporal annotation schemes. In H. Bunt (Ed.), *Proceedings of the Joint ISA-7 Workshop on Interoperable Semantic Annotation, SRSL3 Workshop on Semantic Representation for Spoken Language, and I2MRT Workshop on Multimodal Resources and Tools*, Istanbul, Turkey, pp. 61–68. A satellite workshop of LREC 2012, Istanbul, Turkey.

Mani, I. and J. Pustejovsky (2012). *Interpreting Motion: Grounded Representation for Spatial Language*. Oxford: Oxford University Press.

MITRE (2009). *SpatialML: Annotation Scheme for Marking Spatial Expressions in Natural Language*. The MITRE Corporation. Version 3.1, October 1, 2009, Contact: cdoran@mitre.org.

Pustejovsky, J., R. Ingria, R. Saurí, J. Castaño, J. Littman, R. Gaizauskas, A. Setzer, G. Katz, and I. Mani (2005). The specification language TimeML. In I. Mani, J. Pustejvosky, and R. Gaizauskas (Eds.), *The Language of Time: a Reader*, pp. 545–557. Cambridge: Oxford University Press.

Pustejovsky, J., K. Lee, H. Bunt, and L. Romary (2010). ISO-TimeML: an international standard for semantic annotation. In *Proceedings of LREC 2010*, La Valette, Malta.

Pustejovsky, J., J. Moszkowics, and M. Verhagen (2011). ISOspace: the annotation of spatial information in language. In H. Bunt (Ed.), *Proceedings of the Sixth Joint ISO-ACL/SIGSEM Workshop on Interoperable Semantic Annotation (ISA-6)*, Oxford, England, pp. 1–9.

Pustejovsky, J., J. Moszkowics, and M. Verhagen (2012). The current status of ISO-Space. In H. Bunt (Ed.), *Proceedings of the Joint ISA-7 Workshop on Interoperable Semantic Annotation, SRSL3 Workshop on Semantic Representation for Spoken Language, and I2MRT Workshop on Multimodal Resources and Tools*, Istanbul, Turkey, pp. 23–30. a satellite workshop held in conjunction with LREC 2012, Istanbul, Turkey.

A Flexible Interface Tool for Manual Word Sense Annotation

Steven Neale, João Silva and António Branco
University of Lisbon, Faculty of Sciences
Department of Informatics
{steven.neale, jsilva, antonio.branco}@di.fc.ul.pt

Abstract

This paper introduces LX-SenseAnnotator, a user-friendly interface tool for manual word sense annotation. The demonstration will show how input texts are loaded by the tool, the options available to the annotator for displaying and browsing texts, and how word senses are displayed and manually assigned. The flexibility of LX-SenseAnnotator, including the support of a variety of languages and the handling of pre-processed texts with different tagsets, will also be addressed.

1 Introduction

Annotated corpora are a cornerstone of Natural Language Processing (NLP), supporting the analysis of large quantities of text across a wide variety of contexts (Leech, 2004) and the development and evaluation of processing tools. There has been an increased interest in "high quality linguistic annotations of corpora" at the semantic level, with word senses in particular being "both elusive and central to many areas of NLP" (Passonneau et al., 2012). Sense annotated corpora are useful, for example, as training data for Word Sense Disambiguation (WSD) tools (Agirre and Soroa, 2009), many of which are based on the Princeton WordNet approach to the lexical semantics of nouns, verbs, adjectives and adverbs (Fellbaum, 1998).

This format is widely used to build sense-annotated corpora in a variety of languages—examples include parallel corpora such as the English/Italian MultiSemCor (Bentivogli and Pianta, 2002) and corpora in languages such as Japanese, Bulgarian, German, Polish and many more (Global WordNet Association, 2013). Despite the need for these corpora to train and test new and developing WSD approaches (Wu et al., 2007), tools for manual sense-annotation are not easy to come by.

Finding any information at all about such tools is difficult, and those that are described are often done so in the context of the specific purposes for which they were developed. For example, the tools used to manually annotate the English MASC Corpus (Passonneau et al., 2012) and Chinese Word Sense Annotated Corpus (Wu et al., 2007) both seem intrinsically tied to those particular corpora. Such examples demonstrate the need for a more open, flexible solution for manual word-sense annotation that is more "readily adaptable to different annotation problems"(O'Donnell, 2008).

As part of our research on WSD in Portuguese, we have encountered the need for a more user-friendly way to manually annotate corpora with information about word senses. Based on these requirements, we present LX-SenseAnnotator, a flexible user-interface tool for browsing texts and annotating them with senses pulled from a Princeton-style WordNet. We are using this tool to produce a gold-standard corpus annotated with senses from our Portuguese WordNet for use in our own WSD tasks, and in this paper describe how its usability and flexibility make it well-suited to similar manual annotation tasks using source texts and WordNet-based lexicons in a variety of different languages.

2 Importing Text

The current implementation of LX-SenseAnnotator is designed for the import of text files that have already been tagged and morphologically analyzed (in particular, POS-tagged and lemmatized) in an existing pipeline of NLP tools (Branco and Silva, 2006). POS-tagging in particular makes the separation of the input text according to which words are and are not sense-taggable (as described in the next section) very straightforward. It is of course assumed that the preprocessed tags in the input text have been verified and are correct.

A goal for LX-SenseAnnotator is to support the import of source text in a variety of different formats. The code that currently reads and interprets input text is stored in a stand-alone C++ function, making it easy for the tool to be tuned to allow texts pre-processed using different types of tagsets to be imported depending on the goals of particular users. Coupled with the possibility of reading data from different WordNets (any lexical semantic network in any language that adheres to the Princeton WordNet format can be handled), a wide range of languages and different tagsets for each of those languages can be served by LX-SenseAnnotator.

3 Displaying and Browsing Texts

Before being loaded into the text edit panel, each word from the input text is analyzed according to its need for sense-tagging. In accordance with the Princeton format, nouns, verbs, adjectives and adverbs are separated from the rest of the text as potential candidates for sense-tagging and marked in red, so that they can be easily seen against the rest of the text, which is coloured in a dark blue except for those words that have already been annotated, which are marked in green (Figure 1). An additional search is performed on the words identified as being sense-taggable to ensure that they actually exist in the uploaded WordNet, in this case our Portuguese version—those that do not are also excluded from the red, sense-taggable portions of the text.

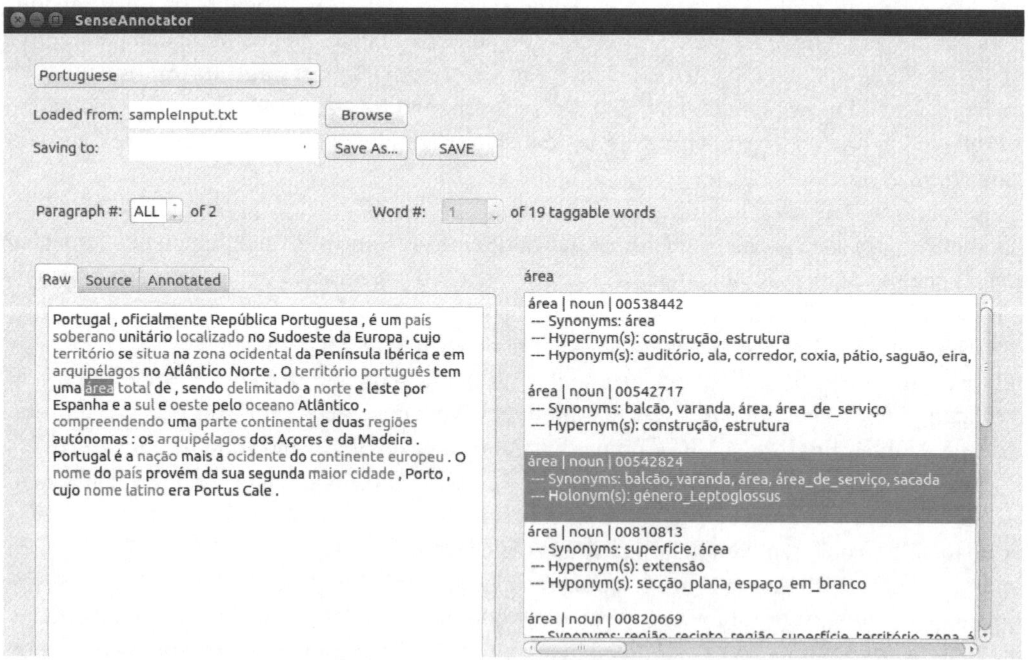

Figure 1: Displaying a list of senses for the word 'área' (English 'area') using LX-SenseAnnotator.

Once the pre-processed text has been uploaded, the human annotator has a choice of viewing it in the text edit panel in three different views—source text, sense-annotated text and raw text—which can be cycled between using a simple tab widget at the top of the panel. The source text tab displays exactly the original source text (complete with all of the tags present in the imported text). The sense-annotated text tab displays the text with all of the tags from the original source text, and appends the newly added sense tags to the text as the human annotator works—essentially, a continually-updated view of how the output file will be.

The raw text tab displays the text in the cleanest view for reading—all of the tags from the original source text, as well as newly added sense tags, are omitted, allowing for easier reading by the annotator (Figure 2). Our own shallow processing tools used to pre-process the text prior to input include a tokenizer which, among other functions, expands Portuguese contracted forms. For example, 'do' is expanded into two separate tokens, 'de+o' ('of+the' in English). To further aid readability, the current Portuguese LX-SenseAnnotator implementation reverses such tokenizations in the raw text tab.

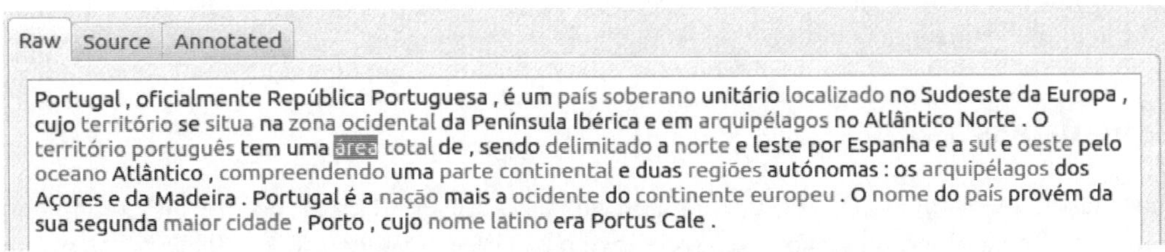

Figure 2: Browsing a text (in Portuguese), with annotated words displayed in green and words yet to be annotated in red.

4 Displaying and Assigning Senses

In any of the three viewing tabs, the annotator can either click on a red, sense-taggable word, or use a scroll-box to browse through the text with currently sense-taggable words. Selecting a word highlights it, and displays the available senses in a separate sense results panel to the right of the text edit panel (Figure 1). The available senses are sourced by querying the presence of the lemma of the selected word in any of the synsets in the index.sense file (limited to the appropriate POS—noun, verb, adjective or adverb). If the word is in a synset, the 8-digit offset of that synset is searched for in the corresponding data file (data.noun, data.verb, etc.) and the results displayed in the right-hand panel as a list of possible options for the selected word.

Information is provided with each sense result to give annotators everything they need to help them decide which sense to assign to a selected word. Using the information from the data (.noun, .verb, etc.) file where the synset was found, each sense result is populated with the main lemma, the POS and the 8-digit offset of the synset. To provide context, this is supplemented with the other words from the synset, which are presented as synonyms, and a selection of the pointers for that synset pulled from the data file (hyper and hyponyms, holonyms, antonyms, entailments, etc.).

After deciding on the most appropriate sense for the selected word, double clicking it in the right-hand sense results panel automatically assigns that sense to the occurence of the word selected in the left-hand text edit panel. In all three viewing tabs, the newly sense-annotated word becomes green, and in the sense-annotated text tab the annotation itself can be seen appended to the selected word. The word is removed from the list of words yet to be annotated, although words which have already been sense-annotated, now displayed in green, can still be selected to allow annotators to assign a different option should they change their mind later.

5 Usability and Flexibility

As mentioned earlier in the paper, LX-SenseAnnotator can read lexical data for any language providing that it adheres to the Princeton WordNet format. The current implementation loads our Portuguese WordNet from a specific directory, from which any number of individual directories containing WordNet-style lexicons can be included and cycled between within the GUI to display senses in different languages. This means that different texts in different languages can be annotated just as easily as each other, simply by loading senses from a different WordNet directory.

Parallel to this is the interpretation of the tags already applied to the input text at the time of import. As the code for handling source text is assigned to a separate, stand-alone C++ function, it is possible to create new classes to interpret tagsets. We plan to further streamline this process by incorporating a simple GUI for annotators to create and edit their own tags, which the program can use to automatically create new versions of the standalone function for interpreting new tagsets in different languages. As the number of supported tagsets grows as a result, so does the flexibility of LX-SenseAnnotator, helping to make manual sense annotation "as flexible for use with common tools and frameworks as possible" (Passonneau et al., 2012).

6 Conclusions

This paper has demonstrated LX-SenseAnnotator, an easy-to-use interface tool for annotating corpora with word-sense data based on a WordNet-style lexicon. There are increasing calls for a "community-wide, collaborative effort to produce open, high quality annotated corpora" that are both "easily accessible and available for use by anyone" (Passonneau et al., 2012). LX-SenseAnnotator can contribute to this effort, offering a flexible, user-friendly platform to build sense-annotated corpora and being particularly suited to creating gold-standard corpora for use in NLP research.

As well as working on improving flexibility in the form of customisable support for tagsets in future updates of LX-SenseAnnotator, there are other elements that are worth taking into consideration. The assumption that the tags in preprocessed input texts are correct has already been mentioned, but specific handling for incorrect tags assigned during preprocessing is important, and providing annotators with the option to highlight and correct such errors using LX-SenseAnnotator would be beneficial. It would also be advantageous if LX-SenseAnnotator were able to handle not just different texts in different languages, but also cases where multiple languages are used within the same text.

We plan to start using the current version of LX-SenseAnnotator to produce a gold-standard sense-annotated corpus in Portuguese for use in our own WSD research, during which process we hope to evaluate the tool from a usability perspective with a team of annotators. We also aim to release LX-SenseAnnotator in the near future as part of the LX-Center (NLX, nd), our existing collection of NLP tools and resources.

Acknowledgements

This work has been undertaken and funded as part of the DP4LT and QTLeap projects.

References

Agirre, E. and A. Soroa (2009). Personalizing PageRank for Word Sense Disambiguation. In *Proceedings of the 12th Conference of the European Chapter of the Association for Computational Linguistics*, EACL '09, Athens, Greece, pp. 33–41. Association for Computational Linguistics.

Bentivogli, L. and E. Pianta (2002). Opportunistic Semantic Tagging. In *Proceedings of the 3rd International Conference on Language Resources and Evaluation*, Las Palmas, Canary Islands, pp. 1401–1406. Association for Computational Linguistics.

Branco, A. and J. R. Silva (2006). A Suite of Shallow Processing Tools for Portuguese: LX-suite. In *Proceedings of the 11th Conference of the European Chapter of the Association for Computational Linguistics: Posters and Demonstrations*, EACL '06, Trento, Italy, pp. 179–182. Association for Computational Linguistics.

Fellbaum, C. (1998). *WordNet: An Electronic Lexical Database*. MIT Press.

Global WordNet Association (2013). WordNet Annotated Corpora. http://globalwordnet.org/wordnet-annotated-corpora/. Accessed: 2015-01-19.

Leech, G. (2004). Adding Linguistic Annotations. In M. Wynne (Ed.), *Developing Linguistic Corpora: A Guide to Good Practice*. AHDS Literature, Languages and Linguistics.

NLX (n.d.). LX-Center: NLX - Natural Language and Speech Group. http://lxcenter.di.fc.ul.pt/home/en/index.html. Accessed: 2015-02-23.

O'Donnell, M. (2008). Demonstration of the UAM CorpusTool for Text and Image Annotation. In *Proceedings of the ACL-08: HLT Demo Session*, Columbus, OH, USA, pp. 13–16. Association for Computational Linguistics.

Passonneau, R. J., C. Baker, C. Fellbaum, and N. Ide (2012). The MASC Word Sense Sentence Corpus. In *Proceedings of the 8th International Conference on Language Resources and Evaluation*, Istanbul, Turkey. European Language Resources Association.

Wu, Y., P. Jin, T. Guo, and S. Yu (2007). Building Chinese Sense Annotated Corpus with the Help of Software Tools. In *Proceedings of the Linguistic Annotation Workshop*, Prague, Czech Republic, pp. 125–131. Association for Computational Linguistics.

Annotating Attribution Relations across Languages and Genres

Silvia Pareti
University of Edinburgh, UK
Google Inc.
s.pareti@sms.ed.ac.uk

1 Introduction

In Pareti (2012) I presented an approach to the annotation of attribution defining it as a relation intertwined albeit independent from other linguistic levels and phenomena. While a portion of this relation can be identified at the syntactic level (Skadhauge and Hardt, 2005) and part of it can overlap with the argument of discourse connectives (Prasad et al., 2006), attribution is best represented and annotated as a separate level.

The present work will present the results of an inter-annotator agreement study conducted in order to validate the annotation scheme described in previous work (Pareti and Prodanof, 2010). The scheme takes a lexicalised approach to attribution and is an extension and modification of the one adopted in the Penn Discourse TreeBank (PDTB) (Prasad et al., 2006). It comprises a set of elements, identified by the text spans expressing them, and a set of features.

Preliminary applications of the scheme to annotate attribution in different languages (English and Italian) and genres (news, spoken dialogues and mailing thread summaries) will also be presented and discussed.

2 Annotation Scheme Validation

This section describes an inter-annotator agreement study that was conducted in order to evaluate the applicability of the proposed annotation scheme before it was adopted to complete the annotation of the WSJ corpus. The study also verifies the validity of the PDTB derived corpus of attribution relations (ARs) before it was employed for the development and testing of quotation extraction and attribution studies (O'Keefe et al., 2012; Pareti et al., 2013; Almeida et al., 2014).

2.1 Annotation Scheme

The AR is defined as constituted by three main elements. The text span expressing each element is annotated and labelled as:

1. *Content*, i.e. what is attributed: this is usually a clause, but it can range from a single word up to several sentences. Content spans can be discontinuous (Ex.(1)).

2. **Source**, i.e. the entity the content is attributed to: a proper or common noun or a pronoun. The source is annotated together with its modifiers (i.e. adjectives, appositives, relative clauses). Sources might be left implicit, e.g. in case of passive or impersonal constructions.

3. <u>Cue</u>, i.e. the link expressing the relation: an attributional verb or, less frequently, a preposition, a noun, an adverb, an adjective or a punctuation mark. Modifiers of the cue, usually adverbs or negation particles, are also included in the cue span.

(1) *"The Caterpillar people aren't too happy when they see their equipment used like that,"* shrugs **Mr. George**. *"They figure it's not a very good advert."*[1]

Optional information perceived as relevant for the interpretation of the AR, because of completing or contributing to its meaning, can be marked and joined in the relation as SUPPLEMENT. This element was introduced to allow the inclusion of circumstantial information as well as additional sources (informers) (e.g. John knows FROM MARY ...) or recipients (e.g. 'the restaurant manager told MS. LEVINE...'(wsj_1692).

The scheme comprises also six features that have been considered for inclusion into the scheme and were tested through an inter-annotator agreement study. Four features correspond to those included in the PDTB annotation: type (assertion, belief, fact, eventuality), source type (writer, other, arbitrary), determinacy or factuality (factual, non factual) and scopal polarity or scopal change. Two additional features are also included, since they are relevant aspect of an attribution and can affect how the content is perceived: authorial stance and source attitude.

The authorial stance reflects the authorial commitment towards the truth of the AR content, and it is the expression of the reporter's voice (Murphy, 2005) and her beliefs (Diab et al., 2009). The annotation distinguishes between neutral (e.g. say), committed (e.g. admit) or non–committed (e.g. lie, joke) authorial stance. The source attitude reflects whether a sentiment is associated with the attitude the source holds towards the content. The annotation scheme allows for five different values: positive (e.g. beam, hail, brag), negative (e.g. decry, fume, convict), tentative (e.g. believe, ponder, sense), neutral (e.g. report) or other.

2.2 Study Definition

In order to test the annotation scheme and identify problematic aspects, a preliminary inter–annotator agreement study was developed on a sample of the WSJ corpus. This sub–corpus consists of 14 articles, selected in order to present instances of all possible attribution types and feature values. Two experts annotators were independently asked to annotate the articles using the MMAX2 annotation tool (Müller and Strube, 2006), following the instructions provided in the annotation manual.

Since annotators were annotating different text spans, the agreement was calculated using the *agr* metric proposed in Wiebe et al. (2005). The *agr* metric is a directed agreement score that can be applied to relation identification tasks where the annotators do not choose between labels for a given annotation unit, but have to decide whether there is or not a relation and the scope of the text span that is part of it. For two given annotators a and b and the respective set of annotations A and B the annotators performed, the score returns the proportion of annotations A that were also identified by annotator b.

2.3 Inter-anotator Agreement Results

The annotators commonly identified 380 attributions out of the overall 491 ARs they annotated. For the AR identification task, the *agr* metric was 0.87. This value reflects the proportion of commonly annotated relations with respect to the overall relations identified by annotator a and annotator b respectively (i.e. the arithmetic mean of $agr(a||b)$ 0.94 and $agr(b||a)$ 0.80). Higher disagreement correlated with the identification of nested attributions, i.e. ARs that appear within the content span of another AR. If overall 22% of the ARs identified by the annotators were nested, the proportion dropped to 15.5% for the ARs identified by both annotators. Nested ARs represent instead over 44% of the ARs identified only by one annotator.

The agreement with respect to choosing the same boundaries for the text spans to annotate was also evaluated with the *agr* metric. The results (Table 1) are very satisfactory concerning the selection of the spans for the source (.94 *agr*), cue (.97 *agr*) and content (.95 *agr*) elements. Concerning the supplement, there was instead little agreement as to what was relevant to the AR in addition to source, cue and content.

[1]Examples in this paper mark the source span of an attribution in **bold**, the content span in *italics* and the cue span as underlined.

Cue	Source	Content	Supplement
0.97	0.94	0.95	0.37

Table 1: Span selection *agr* metrics.

Features	Raw Agreement	Cohen's Kappa	N Disagreements
Type	0.83	0.64	63
Source	0.95	0.71	19
Scopal change	0.98	0.61	5
Authorial stance	0.94	0.20	21
Source attitude	0.82	0.48	67
Factuality	0.97	0.73	9

Table 2: Raw and Kappa agreement for the feature value selection.

Once having identified an attribution, the annotators were asked to select the values for each of the 6 annotated features. Several issues emerged from this task. Despite very high raw agreement values, the corrected Kappa measure shows a very different picture and results mostly below satisfactory. Only the selection of the source type and the factuality value are above the 0.67 recognised by some literature as the threshold allowing for some tentative conclusions, as discussed in detail by Artstein and Poesio (2008).

2.4 Agreement Discussion

The results of the agreement study allowed to identify some issues concerning the proposed features. In particular, the need for a better definition of the boundaries of each feature value. One of the difficulty in applying the proposed annotation schema originated from the number of elements and features that needed to be considered for the annotation of each attribution. This suggests that by decreasing its complexity, the number of errors could be reduced. The annotation should be therefore split into two separate task: the AR annotation and the feature selection.

For certain decisions, test questions could be a useful strategy to ensure a better convergence of the results, e.g. to determine whether the scope of a negation affects the content (and should be annotated as a scopal change) instead of the AR itself (thus affecting its factuality).

While a redefinition of some of the features and a simplification of the task would help reduce ambiguity, subjectivity and errors, the low agreement is also greatly affected by the imbalanced data. Most features assume one value in the majority of the cases, while some values appear only rarely. This has a detrimental effect on the annotator's concentration and ability to recognise these cases.

It is highly desirable to build a complete resource for attribution studies enriched by relevant features that affect the interpretation and perception of ARs. However, in the light of the inter-annotator agreement study, it was decided to restrict further annotation efforts to the AR span selection and postpone the annotation of the features.

3 Attribution in Italian and English

The scheme for the annotation of ARs was initially applied to Italian news articles, leading to the creation of a pilot corpus of 50 texts, the Italian Attribution Corpus (ItAC) (Pareti and Prodanof, 2010).

Attribution relations in Italian are expressed in a similar way as they are in English, thus the same scheme could be used for both languages. Unlike Italian, however, English can express attribution, to an unspecified source, by means of adverbials (e.g. reportedly, allegedly). These cases nonetheless fit the schema (see Ex.(2)) since sources can be left implicit.

(2) *Olivetti* reportedly *began shipping these tools in 1984.*

Table 3 shows a comparison of the Italian pilot (ItAC) and the English PARC 3.0 AR corpora. Both corpora were annotated with the scheme developed for attribution. Although very different in size, some patterns already emerge. The comparison shows a smaller incidence of ARs per thousand tokens in the Italian corpus. This is more likely due to differences in style between the news corpora or to cultural differences rather than to characteristics of the language.

A much higher proportions of ARs in Italian (around 29%) do not have an associated source span. The proportion of ARs without a source is in English rather small (8%) and mostly due to passive constructions and other expressions concealing the source. These cases have usually been disregarded by attribution extraction studies focusing on the identification of the entity the source refers to, since they do not refer to a specific entity or they refer to an entity that is not possible to identify.

Italian however is a pro-drop language, that is, subject pronoun are usually dropped since a rich verb morphology already includes person-number information and they are therefore superfluous. If we also consider that in PARC 3.0 over 19% of source mentions are pronouns, we can understand why Italian has around 20% more ARs without an explicit source than English. Unlike impersonal or missing AR sources in English, pro-drop sources in Italian usually refer to an entity and should be resolved.

	ItAC	PARC 3.0
Texts	50	2,280
Tokens	37k	1,139k
Toks/Text	740	500
ARs	461	19,712
ARs/text	9.2	8.6
ARs/1k tokens	12.5	17.3
ARs no source	29%	8%

Table 3: Comparison of AR news corpora of Italian (ItAC) and English (PARC 3.0) annotated with the AR scheme described in this work.

Some differences between the two languages emerged also concerning the choice and distribution of verbal cues. In a study comparing attribution in English and Italian opinion articles, Murphy (2005) noted that English commentators used more argumentative and debate seeking verbs while the Italian ones are more authoritative and consensus seeking. By looking at the verb type distribution in the two corpora, it is worth noting the high proportion of attributional 'say' in English, around 50% of all cue verbs, which has no parallel in Italian. This might have to do with a tendency towards using a more neutral language in English as well as with the Italian distaste for repetitions and the use of broad meaning verbs, considered as less educated.

The annotation scheme for attribution could be successfully applied to both English and Italian, since they do not present major differences in the structures they use to express attribution.

Other languages, however, can also express attribution morphologically, e.g. some agglutinative languages like Japanese, Korean and Turkish express reportative evidentiality with verb suffixes and particles. These languages would require more investigation to determine whether adaptations to the annotation scheme are necessary.

4 Cross-genre Applications

While extremely frequent and relevant in news, attribution is not a prerogative of this genre. Very little work exists addressing attribution in other genres and it is almost exclusively limited to narrative. PARC 3.0 already contains texts from different genres, albeit all related to news language. The WSJ files included in the PDTB have been classified into 5 different genres: essays, highlights, letters, errata and news. But what if we try to encode attribution in more distant genres and we take into account different registers and domains? In order to test this, I will present here two preliminary studies we developed, annotating attribution on very different kind of corpora: technical mailing thread summaries and informal telephone spoken dialogues.

	PARC 3.0	SARC	KT-pilot
Genre	News	Dialogue	Thread summaries
Register	Formal	Informal	Informal
Medium	Written	Oral	Written
Tokens	1,139k	16k,2h	75k
ARs	19,712	223	1,766
ARs/1k tokens	9.2	14	23

Table 4: Comparison of AR corpora from different genres annotated with the AR scheme described in this work.

4.1 Attribution in Mailing Thread Summaries

The annotation schema for attribution was applied by Bracchi (2014) to a pilot corpus of mailing thread summaries (KT-pilot) sampled from the Kernel Traffic Summaries of the Linux Kernel Mailing List[2]. The corpus differs not only in genre, but also in register and domain. The summaries report what different people contributed in writing to the discussion. This consists in a back and forth of comments and replies. The register is rather informal and the domain is technical. This corpus is particularly interesting for attribution since it is distant from the news genre, but it is also extremely rich in ARs. The corpus was studied by Duboue (2012), who investigated the varied ways of reporting that could be used in summaries.

While the schema was suitable to encode ARs in this genre, some differences emerged with respect to news texts. Bracchi (2014) reports preliminary analysis concerning the attribution cues. She identifies some characteristics of ARs cues in the KT-pilot, for example the use of acronyms as attribution spans, representing both the source and the cue (e.g. IMHO: 'in my humble opinion', AFAIK:'as far as I know', IMNSHO: 'in my not so humble opinion'). Since the annotation allows for the source and cue element to overlap, these cases can be annotated with the acronym corresponding both to the source and the cue span.

(3) *This* **IMHO** *is a good thing for all Real Time SMP*. (Bracchi, 2014)

As Bracchi (2014) notes, the occurrence of attributional verb cues in the KT-pilot is also more distributed, with 'say' covering only 18% of the cases (compared to around 50% in PARC 3.0) and almost 11% being covered by 'reply', a common verb in the mailing thread summaries but rather low-frequency in news. Moreover, some common verbs, strongly associated with attribution in news language (e.g. declare and support) exhibit in the computer domain of the KT-pilot a preferred other use (e.g. 'declare a variable', 'support a version').

4.2 Attribution in Spoken Dialogues

In Cervone et al. (2014), we investigated attribution in spoken informal telephone dialogues and explored the possibility to apply the proposed annotation scheme to a genre using a different medium of communication. The preliminary corpus (Speech Attribution Relation Corpus (SARC)) was annotated with a modification of the scheme for attribution. The basic scheme, with source, cue and content elements being annotated, could be applied to the dialogues, with the only addition of the 'fading out' category. This category is borrowed from Bolden (2004) to account for additional words whose inclusion in the content is ambiguous. In (4) the part of the content span delimited by square brackets is considered as fading out, since it is uncertain whether it still is part of what was originally uttered.

[2](http://kt.earth.li/kernel-traffic/archives.html)

(4) **I** <u>told</u> him *that I cared a lot about him [because I mean I've always been there for him haven't I]*

Although typical of the spoken medium, where only the beginning of a source shift is signalled, 'fading out' has a parallel in written texts, where syntactic ambiguities can leave the content boundaries unclear as in the bracketed portion of the content in Ex.(5) which could be part of what the workers described as well as a remark the author adds. In PARC 3.0, it was up to the annotators to determine the boundaries of the content for each case, although indication was given as to adopt a minimal approach, thus excluding the ambiguous parts.

(5) **Workers** <u>described</u> *"clouds of blue dust" that hung over parts of the factory*, [even though exhaust fans ventilated the area].

Similarly to news, where the article attribution to its writer is not annotated, in SARC the relation between the speaker and each turn utterance in the dialogue is not annotated as an AR. While a dialogue in fiction or an interview in news articles would be an AR, turns in spoken dialogues are not. The turns are not linguistically expressed, as it is obvious to the participant in a spoken conversation what is uttered by a certain speaker (recognised by the voice or because we can see her speaking or because he is simply the other, the voice on the other side of the phone). The attribution of the text itself is not annotated since it is a meta-textual or extra-textual attribution. SARC annotates instead the ARs within a turn utterance.

Some smaller differences with respect to news derive from SARC being a corpus of spoken and colloquial language. Apart from the use of colloquial attributional expressions such as 'I'm like' or 'she goes' that are not likely to appear in news, there are frequent repetitions and broken sentences. In Ex.(6), the source and cue of the AR are repeated twice. In news language this would normally be a case of nested ARs (i.e. Ellie just said to me yesterday: "She said: 'Oh I'm a bit bored of the snow now mum'"). However, here there is only one AR and only the closest source and cue should be annotated since an AR should have only one cue. Each cue established a different AR (e.g. He thinks and knows that ...) although holding between the same source-content pair. While an AR can have multiple sources, this is intended to represent the case when a content is attributed to more than one source (e.g. 'toy manufacturers and other industrialists') and not twice to the same source.

(6) haven't ye ah God do you know I was just off it now and **Ellie** just <u>said</u> to me yesterday **she** <u>said</u> *oh I'm a bit bored of the snow now mum*

The application of a lexicalized approach to attribution to the spoken medium, proved more problematic. In particular, speech lacks punctuation, which instead plays a crucial role in written texts, allowing the identification of direct quotations and in some cases being the only lexical cue of an AR. In speech dialogues instead, part of the role played by punctuation is taken over by acoustic features. The preliminary analysis reported by Cervone (2014) shows some correlation of acoustic aspects, such as pauses, intensity and pitch, with the content boundaries. In the examples below (Cervone (2014)[p.102]), acoustic features allow to reconstruct the ARs in the dialogue turn in Ex.7a as it is shown in Ex.7b with the help of punctuation.

Moreover, not only the content boundary has to rely on extra-textual clues, but in certain cases, the whole AR is reduced in the text to its content element. In spoken language, cues might be expressed by acoustic features and thus not identifiable from the text alone. In the example (Ex.(7)), "what for a loft" and "I'm not going to do that" are attributed to a different source (mentioned at the beginning of the turn as 'she'). However, the source is left implicit and the cue replaced by acoustic means.

(7) a. she wouldn't I said well but I said at the end of the day I said you could sell your house what for a loft and I said well yes if you really didn't have any money you'd have to sell it for a loft buy something smaller well I'm not going to do that and I thought well then you haven't not got any money then have you it's not really the same thing

b. She wouldn't. I said: "Well but", I said: "At the end of the day", I said: "You could sell your house." "What? For a loft?" And I said: "Well, yes! If you really didn't have any money you'd have to sell it for a loft. Buy something smaller." "Well I'm not going to do that." And I thought: "Well, then you haven't not got any money then, have you?" It's not really the same thing.

4.3 Other Forms of Attribution

Not only in the spoken medium, but also in the web one, attribution can also be expressed in extra-textual ways, thus requiring a partly different encoding. For example, attribution can rely on hypertext, both to express the source and to delimit the content span by embedding in it a link to its source.

In addition, the web can make use of graphical elements to show the source of some text, e.g. by embedding part of another page or showing a tweet as an image. Attribution is also graphically expressed in the comics medium, where sources are drawn and cues are rendered by bubbles enclosing the text and encoding the type of attitude by means of specific shapes and by varying the line thickness or continuity.

Also in academic writing, attribution is expressed in a distinct way, with sources being papers commonly referenced in a strictly encoded way.

5 Conclusion

This papers discusses the validity and applicability of the annotation scheme for attribution relations that was proposed in previous work and adopted to annotate PARC 3.0, a large corpus of attribution built on the WSJ corpus. The scheme was tested with a small inter-annotator agreement study. The results showed relatively high agreement for the identification of an AR and very high agreement, over 90%, for the selection of the source, cue and content spans. On the other hand, there was little agreement for the selection of the attribution features, which suggests that they should be redefined and further tested before being included in the annotation.

The scheme has been applied both to English and Italian news corpora. While some differences between the two languages emerged, in particular the higher incidence of ARs with implicit source in Italian, attribution could be annotated in both languages without modifications to the scheme.

The paper reviews two additional pilot corpora from different genres. These were annotated with ARs in order to test the way attribution is expressed in genres other than news articles. While no substantial differences emerged when annotating mailing list thread summaries, the annotation of informal spoken dialogues posed more challenges. In speech, we identified the presence of acoustic elements reinforcing or even replacing the source and cue of an AR, thus showing that an approach solely based on lexical features is not viable for this genre.

Overall, preliminary applications of the current annotation scheme beyond English news texts showed good flexibility and coverage of the current approach. Nonetheless, in specific cases, some adaptation to different language structures and to different genres would be needed.

References

Almeida, M. S. C., M. B. Almeida, and A. F. T. Martins (2014, April). A joint model for quotation attribution and coreference resolution. In Proceedings of the 14th Conference of the European Chapter of the Association for Computational Linguistics, Gothenburg, Sweden, pp. 39–48. Association for Computational Linguistics.

Artstein, R. and M. Poesio (2008, December). Inter-coder agreement for computational linguistics. Comput. Linguist. 34, 555–596.

Bolden, G. (2004). The quote and beyond: defining boundaries of reported speech in conversational russian. Journal of pragmatics 36(6), 1071–1118.

Bracchi, A. (2014, February). Attribution relation cues across genres: A comparison of verbal and non-verbal cues in news and thread summaries. In The 41st Language at Edinburgh Lunch, Edinburgh, UK, pp. poster.

Cervone, A. (2014). Attribution relations extraction in speech: A lexical-prosodic approach. Master's thesis, Università degli Studi di Pavia, Pavia.

Cervone, A., S. Pareti, P. Bell, I. Prodanof, and T. Caselli (2014, December). Detecting attribution relations in speech. In B. M. e. Roberto Basili, Alessandro Lenci (Ed.), First Italian Conference on Computational Linguistics CLiC-it 2014, Pisa, Italy, pp. poster. Pisa University Press.

Diab, M., L. Levin, T. Mitamura, O. Rambow, V. Prabhakaran, and W. Guo (2009). Committed belief annotation and tagging. In Proceedings of the Third Linguistic Annotation Workshop, pp. 68–73.

Duboue, P. (2012). Extractive email thread summarization: Can we do better than he said she said? INLG 2012, 85.

Müller, C. and M. Strube (2006). Multi-level annotation of linguistic data with MMAX2. In S. Braun, K. Kohn, and J. Mukherjee (Eds.), Corpus Technology and Language Pedagogy: New Resources, New Tools, New Methods, pp. 197–214. Germany: Peter Lang.

Murphy, A. C. (2005). Markers of attribution in English and Italian opinion articles: A comparative corpus-based study. ICAME Journal 29, 131–150.

O'Keefe, T., S. Pareti, J. Curran, I. Koprinska, and M. Honnibal (2012). A sequence labelling approach to quote attribution. In Proceedings of the Conference on Empirical Methods in Natural Language Processing (EMNLP).

Pareti, S. (2012, October). The independent encoding of attribution relations. In Proceedings of the Eight Joint ACL-ISO Workshop on Interoperable Semantic Annotation (ISA-8), Pisa, Italy.

Pareti, S., T. O'Keefe, I. Konstas, J. R. Curran, and I. Koprinska (2013, October). Automatically detecting and attributing indirect quotations. In Proceedings of the 2013 Conference on Empirical Methods in Natural Language Processing, Seattle, Washington, USA, pp. 989–999. Association for Computational Linguistics.

Pareti, S. and I. Prodanof (2010). Annotating attribution relations: Towards an Italian discourse treebank. In N. C. et al. (Ed.), Proceedings of LREC10. European Language Resources Association (ELRA).

Prasad, R., N. Dinesh, A. Lee, A. Joshi, and B. Webber (2006). Annotating attribution in the Penn Discourse TreeBank. In Proceedings of the Workshop on Sentiment and Subjectivity in Text, SST '06, pp. 31–38.

Skadhauge, P. R. and D. Hardt (2005). Syntactic identification of attribution in the RST treebank. In Proceedings of the Sixth International Workshop on Linguistically Interpreted Corpora.

Wiebe, J., T. Wilson, and C. Cardie (2005). Annotating expressions of opinions and emotions in language. Language Resources and Evaluation 39, 165–210.

Semantic Relations in Discourse: The Current State of ISO 24617-8

Rashmi Prasad* and Harry Bunt**
*Department of Health Informatics and Administration,
University of Wisconsin-Milwaukee, Milwaukee, USA
**Tilburg Center for Cognition and Communication (TiCC),
Tilburg University, Tilburg, Netherlands
prasadr@uwm.edu bunt@uvt.nl

Abstract

This paper describes some of the research conducted with the aim to develop a proposal for an ISO standard for the annotation of semantic relations in discourse. A range of theoretical approaches and annotation efforts were analysed for their commonalities and their differences, in order to define a clear delineation of the scope of the ISO effort and to give it a solid theoretical and empirical basis. A set of 20 *core* discourse relations was identified as indispensible for an annotation standard, and these relations were provided with clear definitions and illustrative examples from existing corpora. The ISO principles for linguistic annotation in general and semantic annotation in particular were applied to design a markup language (DRelML) for discourse relation annotation.

1 Introduction

The last decade has seen a proliferation of linguistically annotated corpora coding many phenomena in support of empirical natural language research – both computational and theoretical. In the realm of discourse (which for the purposes of this paper is taken to include dialogue as well), a surge of interest in discourse processing has led to the development of several corpora annotated for discourse relations, for example, causal, contrastive and temporal relations. Discourse relations, also called 'coherence relations' or 'rhetorical relations', may be expressed explicitly or implicitly, and they convey meaning that is key to an understanding of the discourse, beyond the meaning conveyed by individual clauses and sentences. The types of abstract semantic objects connected by discourse relations include events, states, conditions and dialogue acts, that are typically expressed as sentences, but they can also be smaller or larger units (clauses, paragraphs, dialogue segments), and they may also occur between abstract objects not explicitly realized but inferrable from semantic content. Discourse relations and discourse structure are key ingredients for NLP tasks such as summarization (Marcu, 2000; Louis et al., 2010), complex question answering (Verberne et al., 2007), and natural language generation (McKeown, 1985; Hovy, 1993; Prasad et al., 2005) and there are now several international and collaborative efforts to create annotated resources of discourse relations, across languages as well as across genres, to support the development of such applications.

This paper describes some of the research conducted with the aim to develop a proposal for an ISO standard for the annotation of semantic relations in discourse. A range of theoretical approaches and annotation efforts were analysed for their commonalities and their differences, in order to define a clear delineation of the scope of the ISO effort and to give it a solid theoretical and empirical basis. A set of 20 *core* discourse relations was identified as indispensible for an annotation standard, and these relations were provided with clear definitions and illustrative examples from existing corpora. The ISO principles for linguistic annotation in general and semantic annotation in particular were applied to design a markup language (DRelML) for discourse relation annotation. The proposed standard is restricted to the annotation of 'local' discourse relations between two abstract objects, in that these relations are annotated independently of other relations in the same text or dialogue. The standard does not consider higher-level discourse structure representations which would involve linking relations between units whose local relations are annotated, and would form a linking structure for an entire discourse. The standard is moreover restricted to strictly informational relations, to the exclusion of, for example, presentational relations, which concern the way in which a text is presented to its readers or the way in which speakers structure their contributions in spoken dialogue. In this paper, we present the key aspects of the proposed standard.

2 Basic concepts

2.1 Discourse relations and their realization

A major aspect of understanding a text comes from understanding how the events, states, conditions, beliefs, dialogue acts and other types of abstract objects mentioned in the discourse are related to each other by relations such as Cause, Contrast, and Condition. Examples (1-3), taken from the Wall Street Journal corpus, illustrate the Cause relation realized in different ways (shown underlined) in a text – as an explicit subordinating conjunction in (1), as an explicit expression not belonging to any well-defined syntactic class in (2), and as an implicit relation in (3). In each case, the two abstract object arguments of the discourse relation are highighlighted, in italics and boldface, respectively.

(1) Mr. Taft, who is also president of Taft Broadcasting Co., said *he bought the shares* because **he keeps a utility account at the brokerage firm of Salomon Brothers Inc., which had recommended the stock as a good buy**.

(2) *But a strong level of investor withdrawal is much more unlikely this time around*, fund managers said. A major reason is **that investors already have sharply scaled back their purchases of stock funds since Black Monday**.

(3) *Some have raised their cash positions to record levels.* (Implicit (because)) **High cash positions help buffer a fund when the market falls**.

Existing frameworks for representing discourse relations differ along several lines. This section provides a comparison of the most important frameworks, focusing on those that have been used as the basis for annotating discourse relations in corpora, in particular, the theory of discourse coherence developed by Hobbs (Hobbs, 1990), Rhetorical Structure Theory (Mann and Thompson, 1988), the cognitive account of coherence relations by Sanders et al (Sanders et al., 1992), Segmented Discourse Representation Theory (Asher and Lascarides, 2003), and the annotation framework of the Penn Discourse Treebank (Prasad et al., 2008, 2014), which is loosely based on DLTAG (Webber et al., 2003). The comparison highlights and discusses the differences that are considered relevant for developing a pivot representation in ISO SemAF-DRel. For each issue, the discussion is followed by the position adopted in the ISO standard. The section ends with a summary of the key concepts used in the ISO SemAF-DRel specification, and the ISO SemAF-DRel metamodel.

2.2 Representation of discourse structure

One difference between frameworks concerns the representation of structure. For example, the RST Bank (Carlson et al., 2003), based on Rhetorical Structure Theory (Mann and Thompson, 1988), assumes a tree representation to subsume the complete text of the discourse. The Discourse Graphbank (Wolf and Gibson, 2005), based on Hobbs' theory of discourse (Hobbs, 1990), allows for general graphs that allow multiple parents and crossing, and the DISCOR corpus (Reese et al., 2007) and ANNODIS corpus (Afantenos et al., 2012), based on Segmented Discourse Representation Theory (SDRT) (Asher and Lascarides, 2003), allow directed acyclic graphs that allow for multiple parents, but not for crossing. There are also frameworks that are pre-theoretical or theory-neutral with respect to discourse structure, including the PDTB (Prasad et al., 2008), based loosely on DLTAG (Webber et al., 2003), and DiscAn

(Sanders and Scholman, 2012), based on (Sanders et al., 1992). In both of these, individual relations along with their arguments are annotated without being combined to form a structure that encompasses the entire text. *The ISO standard takes a pre-theoretical stance involving low-level annotation of discourse; individual relations can then be annotated further to project a higher-level tree or graph structure, depending on one's theoretical preferences.* From the point of view of interoperability, low-level annotation can serve as a pivot representation when comparing annotations based on different theories.

2.3 Semantic description of discourse relations

Some frameworks, such as SDRT, Hobb's theory, PDTB, and Sanders et al's theory, describe the meaning of discourse relations in 'informational' terms, i.e., in terms of the content of the arguments; RST, on the other hand, provides definitions in terms of the intended effects on the hearer/reader. In many cases it is possible to cast one type of definition into the other. *In the ISO standard, discourse relation meaning is described in informational terms*, with the idea that a mapping can be created from the ISO core relations to those present in various existing classifications, including those that define relations in intentional terms. These mappings will be provided in the ISO document for the standard.

2.4 Pragmatic variants of discourse relations

With the exception of Hobbs (1990), all frameworks distinguish relations when one or both of the arguments involve an implicit belief or a dialogue act that takes scope over the semantic content of the argument. This is motivated by examples like (4), where John's sending of the message did not cause him to be absent from work, but rather that it caused the speaker/writer to say that John is not at work. Similarly, in (5), an explanation is provided not for the content of the question but for the questioning act itself.

(4) John is not at work today, because he sent me a message to say he was sick.

(5) What are you doing tonight? Because there's a good movie on.

This distinction is known in the literature as the 'semantic-pragmatic' distinction in Van Dijk (1979), Sanders et al. (1992), and Miltsakaki et al. (2008); as the 'internal-external' distinction in Halliday and Hasan (1976) and Martin (1992); as the 'ideational-pragmatic' distinction in Redeker (1990); and as the 'content-metatalk' distinction in SDRT (Asher and Lascarides, 2003). Some frameworks, such as that of Sanders et al. (1992), allow this distinction for all relation types; others, like the PDTB and RST only admit it for some. In the absence of *a priori* reasons for a restriction to only some relation types, we believe that the choice should in the end be determined by what is observed in corpus data. *In the ISO scheme, therefore, the 'semantic-pragmatic' distinction is allowed for all relation types*, in accordance with the general aim of not being overly restrictive in the absence of well-defined criteria. *However, the ISO scheme does not encode this distinction on the relation, but on the arguments of the relation*, because in all cases involving the inference of an implicit belief or dialogue act, what is different is not the relation itself, but rather that the arguments require an inference of a belief or dialogue act that is *implicit* in the text and that, when factored into the interpretation, changes the status of the abstract objects between which the relation holds.

2.5 Hierarchical classification of discourse relations

All existing frameworks group discourse relations together to a greater or lesser degree, but they differ in how the groupings are made. For example, while PDTB groups Concession together with Contrast under the broader Comparison class, Sanders et al. place Concession under the Negative Causal relation group but Contrast under the Negative Additive group. Reconciliation of these groupings across the frameworks is difficult, since they arise from differences in what is taken to count as semantic closeness. *The solution adopted in the ISO scheme is to initially provide a 'flat' set of core relations.* A major advantage of a flat set is that it can serve as a pivot representation between frameworks, especially between those that groups relations differently. In the full ISO-DRel standard document, we have provided mappings between ISO-Drel relations and each of the different annotations frameworks taken into consideration here. A disadvantage, especially for the specific set of relations developed here, is that in some cases, an ISO relation can turn out to be a more general case of more fine-grained relations in some framework. However, we note that the ISO core relation set is part of an ongoing effort and we envisage further extensions to the relation set. Furthermore, an extension to the scheme that provides a well-motivated taxonomical structure is planned to be elaborated in concertation with the multilingual European TextLink project (`http://textlinkcost.wix.com/textlink`).

2.6 Representation of (a)symmetry of relations

Virtually all existing frameworks embody a representation of whether a discourse relation is symmetric or asymmetric, that is, for a given relation REL and its arguments A and B, whether (REL, A, B) is equivalent to (REL, B, A). For example, the Contrast relation is symmetric whereas the Cause relation is asymmetric. Frameworks differ in how this distinction is represented in their annotation scheme. Most classifications encode asymmetry in terms of the textual linear ordering and/or syntax of the argument realizations. Thus, in Sanders et al's classification, where the argument span ordering is one of the 'cognitive' primitives underlying the scheme, the relation Cause-Consequence captures the 'basic' order for the semantic causal relation, with the cause appearing before the effect, whereas the relation Consequence-Cause is used for the reversed order of the arguments. In the PDTB, argument spans are named Arg1 and Arg2 according to syntactic criteria, including linear order, and the asymmetrical relations are defined in terms of the Arg1 and Arg2 labels (for example, the relation Cause:Reason has Arg2 as the cause and Arg1 as the effect, while the relation Cause:Result has Arg1 as the cause and Arg2 as the effect.

In the ISO scheme, annotations abstract over the linear ordering for argument realizations, since this is not a semantic distinction. Instead, asymmetry is represented by specifying the argument roles in the definition of each relation. Arguments are named Arg1 and Arg2, but they bear relation-specific semantic roles. For example, in the Cause relation defined as 'Arg1 serves as an explanation for Arg2' (see Table 1), the text span named Arg1 will be the one that provides the reason in the Cause relation, irrespective of linear order or any other syntactic consideration. Similarly, Arg2 will always correspond to what constitutes the result in the relation. This representation can be effectively mapped to other schemes for representing asymmetry. It is important to note that this representation in no way obfuscates the differences in linear ordering of the arguments, which can be easily determined by pairing the argument role annotations with the text span annotations. Linear ordering has a bearing for claims that different versions of an asymmetric relation may not have the same linguistic constraints, for example, in terms of linguistic predictions for the following discourse (Asher et al., 2007).

2.7 Relative importance of arguments for text meaning/structure

Some frameworks, namely RST, Hobbs' theory, and SDRT distinguish relations or arguments in terms of their 'relative importance' for the meaning or structure of the text as a whole. In RST, one argument of an asymmetric relation is labeled the 'nucleus', whereas the other is labeled 'satellite' (Mann and Thompson (1988), Pg. 266). Hobbs (1990) has a similar approach, using the term 'dominance', with the goal of deriving a single assertion from a discourse relation that connects two segments, and distinguishing relations in terms of how this single assertion should be derived. In subordinating relations, in particular, the assertion associated with the relation is obtained from the 'dominant' segment, as specified in the relation definitions. SDRT, on the other hand, classifies a relation as 'subordinating' or 'coordinating' depending on what structural configuration the arguments create in the discourse graph (Asher and Vieu, 2005). *In the ISO scheme, the relative role of arguments for the text (meaning or structure) as a whole is not represented directly*, but because of the explicit identification of the roles of the arguments in each relation definition, such a layer of representation can be derived using the relation-specific argument roles. For example, for the Cause relation, a mapping from ISO categories to RST categories would label the Arg1 (corresponding to the reason) argument as the satellite and the Arg2 (corresponding to the result) argument as the nucleus.

2.8 Syntactic form, extent and (non-)adjacency of arguments

Concerning the kinds of syntactic forms the realization of an argument can have, all frameworks agree that the typical realization of an argument is as a clause, but some allow for certain non-clausal phrases as well. This issue gets very complicated when a wide range of languages is considered. *In the ISO standard, constraints are placed on the semantic nature of arguments rather than on their syntactic form. That is, an argument of a discourse relation must denote a certain type of abstract object.*

Two related issues have to do with how complex the realizations of arguments can be syntactically, and whether arguments need to be adjacent in the discourse. With respect to complexity, all frameworks allow for argument realizations to be arbitrarily complex, composed of multiple clauses in coordination or subordinate relations, as well as multiple sentences, as long as they are required for interpreting the relation in which they participate. In some cases, such as the PDTB, further stipulations are made to the effect that argument realizations must contain the 'minimal' amount of information needed to interpret the relation. With respect to adjacency, some frameworks, such as RST, require the related arguments to be realized by textually adjacent phrases, whereas others, such as the PDTB, impose this constraint only for implicit discourse relations. To a large extent, these differences arise because of differences in assumptions about the global structure of a text, which are, then, naturally reflected in the annotation. As with syntactic form, it is difficult to reconcile these differences. *The ISO scheme remains neutral on this issue and does not specify any constraints on the extent or adjacency of argument realizations.*[1]

2.9 Summary: Assumptions of ISO standard under development

In summary, the following provides the basic concepts underlying the ISO standard under development for representing and annotating discourse relations.

- A discourse relation is a relation expressed in text/dialogue between abstract objects, such as events, states, conditions, and dialogue acts.
- Discourse relations can be expressed explicitly in text/speech or can be implicit. The annotation of implicit relations may optionally include the specification of a connective that could express the inferred relation.
- A discourse relation takes two and only two arguments. But arguments can be shared by different relations.
- The meaning of discourse relations is described in informational terms.
- Pragmatic aspects of meaning involving beliefs and dialogue acts as one or both of the arguments are represented as a property of arguments, rather than of discourse relations, and come into play only when the belief or dialogue act is implicit.
- Discourse relations are categorized as a flat set of relations.
- Annotations are at a low level; the ISO scheme is agnostic towards the nature of the global structure of a text or dialogue.
- Asymmetrical relations are represented with relation-specific argument role labels.
- The relative importance of a relation's arguments with respect to the text as a whole is not represented as such.
- No a priori assumptions are made concerning constraints on syntactic form, syntactic complexity, or textual adjacency of expressions that may realize the arguments of a discourse relation.

These choices are reflected in the metamodel of the ISO annotation scheme shown in Figure 1.

[1] Despite the flexibility for these argument features in the current ISO model, we note that for a fully interoperable annotation scheme, it is important for a consensus to be established for well-defined constraints on arguments.

3 The Annotation of Discourse Relations in DRelML

3.1 Overview

The Discourse Relations Markup Language DRelML is designed in accordance with ISO 24617-6, Principles of semantic annotation[2], which implements the distinction between annotations and representations that is made in the Linguistic Annotation Framework (ISO 24612). Accordingly, the definition of an annotation language consists of three parts:

1. an abstract syntax, which specifies a class of annotation structures in accordance with a certain conceptual view, expressed in a given metamodel;
2. a formal semantics, describing the meaning of the annotation structures defined by the abstract syntax;
3. a concrete syntax, specifying a reference format for representing the annotation structures defined by the abstract syntax.

Abstract and concrete syntax are related through the requirements that the concrete syntax is *complete* and *unambiguous* relative to the abstract syntax. Completeness means that the concrete syntax defines a representation for every structure defined by the abstract syntax; unambiguity means that every expression defined by the concrete syntax represents one and only one structure defined by the abstract syntax. A representation format defined by a concrete syntax which has these two properties is called an *ideal* representation format. An important aspect of this approach is that *any ideal representation format is convertible through a meaning-preserving mapping to any other ideal representation format* (including the GrAF format defined by Ide and Suderman (2007), as shown in (Ide and Bunt, 2010)).

In this section we present the metamodel that expresses the conceptual view underlying DRelML and outline its abstract and concrete syntax. The semantics of DRelML annotations, which is defined through a translation into discourse representation structures (DRSs), is outlined in the appendix.

Note that annotators only have to deal with the *concrete* DRelML syntax; the underlying abstract syntax is relevant mainly for establishing possible mappings between DRelML and other annotation schemes; the semantics is relevant for the extraction of content from DRelML annotated resources.

3.2 Metamodel

Of central importance in the annotation of discourse relations are evidently the relations and their arguments, and they take central stage in the metamodel shown in Figure 1. Discourse relations are linked to relation arguments through argument roles. The arguments themselves can be of various types, as indicated by the link from relation arguments to argument types. This standard assumes that two types of arguments have to be distinguished (possibly with subtypes): 'situations', which include eventualities (events, states, processes,...), facts, conditions, as well as negated eventualities (as in *"Mary smiled at John, but the didn't smile back"*), and dialogue acts involved in 'pragmatic' interpretations of discourse relations (as in *"Carl is a fool; he beats his wife"*).

The assumption made in the present standard that all discourse relations are binary is represented in the metamodel by the number '2' at the tip of the arrow from discourse relations to arguments.

The arguments of a discourse relation are always realized explicitly in the primary data; this is reflected by the fact that each argument is related to a markable, which in turn is associated with a segment of primary data. The fact that a discourse relation can be explicit or implicit is reflected in the indication '0..1' at the tip of the arrow from discourse relations to markables.

The dotted arrows at the bottom indicate possible links to another layer of annotation, concerned with the identification of the source to which a discourse relation or (one or both of) its arguments may be attributed.

[2]See Bunt (2015) for a summary description of ISO 24617-6.

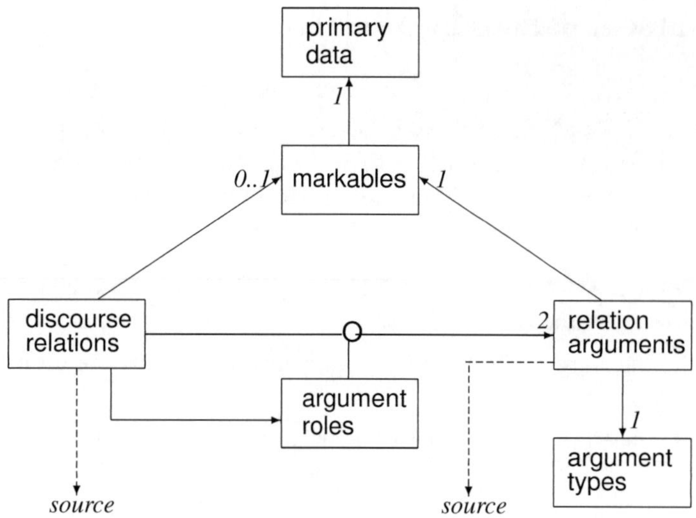

Figure 1: Metamodel for the annotation of discourse relations.

3.3 Abstract syntax

The abstract syntax of DRelML consists of (a) a 'conceptual inventory', i.e. a specification of the concepts from which annotations are built up, and (b) a specification of the possible ways of combining these elements into conceptual structures, called 'annotation structures'.

Conceptual inventory The conceptual inventory of DRelML contains the concepts that form the ingredients for building annotation structures:

1. D, a set of discourse relations.
2. R, a set of argument roles for discourse relations.
3. A function σ from R to $D \times D$ which assigns two argument roles to every discourse relation;
4. M, a set of markables that identify the segments of primary data to be marked up in a given annotation task. Different from the other ingredients of the conceptual inventory, this set is specific for an annotation task.
5. T, a set of argument types, including the types 'situation' and 'dialogue act'.

Annotation structures An annotation structure is a set of entity structures, which contain semantic information about a region of primary data, and link structures, which describe a semantic relation between two such regions.

An entity structure is either (1) a relation entity structure, which is a pair $\langle m_i, r_j \rangle$ consisting of a markable m_i, and a discourse relation r_j, or (2) an argument entity structure, which is a pair $\langle m_k, t \rangle$ consisting of a markable and an argument type.

A link structure captures the information that an argument participates in a discourse relation in a certain role, such as a triple $\langle \rho_{cause}, \varepsilon, \alpha \rangle$ consisting of a relation entity structure, an argument entity structure, and an argument role.

3.4 Concrete syntax

An XML-based representation format can be defined by introducing XML elements, attributes and values corresponding to the components of the abstract syntax. This means the specification of a vocabulary corresponding to the conceptual inventory and the definition of representation structures for the entity structures and link structures of the abstract syntax.

Vocabulary In an XML-based concrete syntax, the n-tuples of concepts that form annotation structures are represented by lists of attribute-value pairs that make up XML elements. In an XML element the meaning of a component is indicated by the name of an attribute (rather than by the position in a conceptal n-tuple), The vocabulary of DRelML therefore contains names of attributes that represent the meaning of a position in an annotation structure, and values that name the corresponding concepts. In addition, DRelML exploits the possibility of using semantically insignificant optional parts in its representations in allowing the insertion of connective expressions in the representation of implicit discourse relations (as in PDTB annotations).

Representation structures The representation of an annotation structure is a list of the representations of its entity structures and link structures. These representation are defined as follows:

1. A relation entity structure is represented by an XML element called dRel, with the following attributes:
   - xml:id, whose value specifies a unique identifier (unique within the annotation structure);
   - target, whose value represents a markable that identifies a location in the text where a discourse relation is mentioned;
   - rel, whose value names a discourse relation.
2. An argument entity structure is represented by an XML element 'drArg', with the following attributes:
   - xml:id, whose value specifies a unique identifier;
   - target, whose value represents a markable that identifies a location in the text where a discourse relation is mentioned;
   - argType, whose value specifies an argument type.
3. A link structure containing an implicit discourse relation is represented by an XML element called implRel, which has the following attributes:
   - xml:id, whose value specifies a unique identifier;
   - rel, whose value names a discourse relation;
   - markables, whose value is a sequence of two markables, identifying the arguments of an occurrence of the implicit discourse relation;
   - disConn, whose value represents a connective, that could be inserted for an implicit discourse relation (optional).
4. A link structure containing an explicit discourse relation is represented by an XML element called drLink, which has the following attributes:
   - rel, whose value represents a relation entity structure;
   - arg, whose value is a drArg element representing an argument of a discourse relation;
   - role, whose value represents a semantic role in a discourse relation.

The following example shows the DRelML annotation representation constructed by this concrete syntax as well as the corresponding semantics. Note that both arguments of the Cause relation in this example are characterised as 'situation', rather than 'dialogue act' (or 'belief') in order to indicate the 'semantic' interpretation of the relation. The treatment of a 'pragmatic' Cause relation is considered in the appendix, which also provides more details on the derivation of the semantics from the annotation structures underlying the representations considered here.

(6) a. Carl is crazy, because he got his father's bad genes.

b. [r1] <dRel xml:id="r1" target="#m2" rel="cause"/>
[a1] <drArg xml:id="s2" target="#m3" argType="situation"/>
[a2] <drArg xml:id="s1" target="#m1" argType="situation"/>
[L1] <drLink rel="#r1" arg="s2" role="arg1"/>
[L2] <drLink rel="#r1" arg="s1" role="arg2"/>

c.

r, e1, e2
cause(r) situation(e1) result(r,e1) situation(e2) reason(r,e2)

4 ISO Core Discourse Relations

The ISO set of core discourse relations is at a level of granularity that is neither too broad nor too fine-grained. Semantic equivalences are established with five well-known semantic taxonomies for discourse relations: PDTB (Miltsakaki et al., 2008); Kehler's theory of discourse coherence (Kehler, 1995), which is itself largely based on Hobbs' work (Hobbs, 1990), Rhetorical Structure Theory (Mann and Thompson, 1988), SDRT (Asher and Lascarides, 2003) and the taxonomy of Sanders et al. (1992). It also draws on the experiences with discourse relation annotation in multiple languages and genres (Carlson et al., 2003; Wolf and Gibson, 2005; Prasad et al., 2008; Oza et al., 2009; Prasad et al., 2011; Zufferey et al., 2012; Zhou and Xue, 2012; Mladová et al., 2008; Afantenos et al., 2012; Sanders and Scholman, 2012), among others.

	ISO DRel	Symmetry	Relation and Argument-Role Definitions
1.	Cause	Asymmetric	Arg1 serves as an explanation for Arg2.
2.	Condition	Asymmetric	Arg1 is an unrealized situation which, when realized, would lead to Arg2.
3.	Negative Condition	Asymmetric	Arg1 is an unrealized situation which, when not realized, would lead to Arg2.
4.	Purpose	Asymmetric	Arg1 serves to enable Arg2.
5.	Manner	Asymmetric	Arg1 describes how Arg2 comes about or occurs
6.	Concession	Asymmetric	An expected causal relation between Arg1 and Arg2, where Arg1 is expected to cause Arg2, is cancelled or denied by Arg2.
7.	Contrast	Symmetric	One or more differences between Arg1 and Arg2 are highlighted with respect to what each predicates as a whole or to some entities they mention.
8.	Exception	Asymmetric	Arg1 evokes a set of circumstances in which the described situation holds, while Arg2 indicates one or more instances where it doesnt.
9.	Similarity	Symmetric	One or more similarities between Arg1 and Arg2 are highlighted with respect to what each predicates as a whole or to some entities they mention.
10.	Substitution	Asymmetric	Arg1 and Arg2 are alternatives, with B being the favored or chosen alternative.
11.	Conjunction	Symmetric	Both Arg1 and Arg2 bear the same relation to some other situation evoked in the discourse. Their conjunction indicates that they are doing the same thing with respect to that situation, or are doing it together.
12.	Disjunction	Symmetric	Arg1 and Arg2 are alternatives, with either one or both holding
13.	Exemplification	Asymmetric	Arg1 evokes a set of circumstances in which the described situation holds, and Arg2 instantiates an instance of the set.
14.	Elaboration	Asymmetric	Both Arg1 and Arg2 describe the same situation, but in more or less detail.
15.	Restatement	Symmetric	Both Arg1 and Arg2 describe the same situation, but from different perspectives.
16.	Synchrony	Symmetric	Some degree of temporal overlap exists between Arg1 and Arg2. All forms of overlap are included.
17.	Asynchrony	Asymmetric	Arg1 temporally precedes Arg2.
18.	Expansion	Asymmetric	Arg2 provides further description about some entity or entities in Arg1, expanding the narrative forward of which Arg1 is a part, or expanding on the setting relevant for interpreting Arg1.
19.	Functional dependence	Asymmetric	Arg2 is a dialogue act whose semantic content is, due to the dialogue act type, dependent on that of the dialogue act Arg1, that occurred earlier in the discourse.
20.	Feedback dependence	Asymmetric	Arg2 is a feedback act that provides or elicits information about the processing of Arg1, which occurred earlier in the discourse, by one of the dialogue participants.

Table 1: ISO set of core discourse relations

Table 1 presents the proposed set of core ISO discourse relations. The level of granularity is motivated by the consideration that these relations cover what has been more or less successfully implemented in various annotation efforts to date. However, this set is by no means fixed and can be augmented if necessary. As discussed in Section 2.6, the semantic roles of the two arguments are built into the definition of each relation. For lack of space, examples of only a few relations are given below. For examples of other relations, the reader is referred to the ISO document.

1. Cause: **Arg1** serves as an explanation for *Arg2*.

   a) Perhaps because **they won**, *Mr. Bork's attackers come through more vividly than his defenders.*

   b) *Sears is negotiating to refinance its Sears Tower for close to $850 million*, sources said. (Implicit=because) **The retailer was unable to find a buyer for the building**.

   c) **Now, though, enormous costs for earthquake relief will pile on top of outstanding costs for hurricane relief**. "That obviously means *that we won't have enough for all of the emergencies that are now facing us, and we will have to consider appropriate requests for follow-on funding,"* Mr. Fitzwater said.

   d) *The nations of southern Africa know a lot about managing elephants*; (Implicit=as) **their herds are thriving**.

2. Condition: **Arg1** is an unrealized situation which, when realized, would lead to *Arg2*.

   a) But some bond market analysts said *that could quickly change* if **property casualty insurance companies scramble to sell portions of their municipal portfolios to raise cash to pay damage claims**.

   b) If **anyone has difficulty imagining a world in which history went merrily on without us**, *Mr. Gould sketches several*.

3. Functional dependence: **Arg2** is a dialogue act whose semantic content is, due to its communicative function, on that of another dialogue act, *Arg1*, that occurred earlier in the discourse.

   a) *A: What newspapers do you read?* [Question]
   B: I read uh the local newspaper, and I also try and read one of the uh major dailies like the Chicago Tribune, or the New York Times or something like that [Answer]

   b) *B: I really like NPR a lot* [Inform]
   A: Yeah that?s pretty good [Agreement]

4. Feedback dependence: **Arg2** is a feedback act, i.e. a dialogue act that provides or elicits information about the processing of something said earlier by one of the dialogue participants; *Arg1* is the (sequence of) dialogue acts – or their semantic content, or their realisation – whose processing is considered.

   a) *A: go south and you'll pass some cliffs on your right*
   B: okay
   A: and keep going down south
   B: mmhmm

   b) *A: we are going to go due south straight south and then we're going to turn straight back round and head north past an old mill on the right hand side*
   B: due south and then back up again

5 Conclusions

In this paper we have summarized some of the research conducted with the aim to formulate a proposal for an ISO standard for the annotation of semantic relations in discourse. On the basis of an analysis of a range of theoretical approaches and annotation efforts a clear delineation of the scope of the ISO effort was made, restricting the effort for example to local, low-level relations with a solid theoretical and empirical basis. The ISO principles for linguistic annotation in general and semantic annotation in particular were applied to design the markup language DRelML for discourse relation annotation. Future work will aim to remove some of the restrictions adopted so far, in particular aiming to develop a well-motivated taxonomy of discourse relations in collaboration with the European TextLink project.

Although the proposal is based on existing practices and experiences such as the PDTB, the ISO scheme will need to be validated by converting existing annotations to those of the ISO scheme, as well as applying the scheme in annotation campaigns.

Acknowledgement

This work was partially supported by NSF grant IIS-1421067.

References

Afantenos, S., N. Asher, F. Benamara, M. Bras, C. Fabre, L.-M. Ho-Dac, A. L. Draoulec, P. Muller, M.-P. Pry-Woodley, L. Prvot, J. Rebeyrolle, L. Tanguy, M. Vergez-Couret, and L. Vieu (2012). An empirical resource for discovering cognitive principles of discourse organisation: the ANNODIS corpus. In *Proceedings of the Eight International Conference on Language Resources and Evaluation (LREC'12)*.

Asher, N. and A. Lascarides (2003). *Logics of conversation*. Cambridge University Press.

Asher, N., L. Prévot, and L. Vieu (2007). Setting the background in discourse. *Discours. Revue de linguistique, psycholinguistique et informatique* (1).

Asher, N. and L. Vieu (2005). Subordinating and coordinating discourse relations. *Lingua 115*(4), 591–610.

Bunt, H. (2014). Annotations that effectively contribute to semantic interpretation. In *Computing meaning*, pp. 49–69. Springer.

Bunt, H. (2015). On the principles of interoperable semantic annotation. In *Proceedings of the 11th Joint ACL-ISO Workshop on Interoperable Semantic Annotation*, pp. 1–13.

Carlson, L., D. Marcu, and M. E. Okurowski (2003). Building a discourse-tagged corpus in the framework of Rhetorical Structure Theory. In J. van Kuppevelt and R. Smith (Eds.), *Current Directions in Discourse and Dialogue*, pp. 85–112. Kluwer Academic Publishers.

Halliday, M. A. K. and R. Hasan (1976). *Cohesion in English*. London: Longman.

Hobbs, J. R. (1990). *Literature and Cognition*. Menlo Park, Cal.: CSLI/SRI.

Hovy, E. H. (1993). Automated discourse generation using discourse structure relations. *Artificial Intelligence 63*, 341–385.

Ide, N. and H. Bunt (2010). Anatomy of annotation schemes: mapping to graf. In *Proceedings of the Fourth Linguistic Annotation Workshop*, pp. 247–255. Association for Computational Linguistics.

Ide, N. and K. Suderman (2007). Graf: A graph-based format for linguistic annotations. In *proceedings of the Linguistic Annotation Workshop*, pp. 1–8. Association for Computational Linguistics.

Kehler, A. (1995). *Interpreting Cohesive Forms in the Context of Discourse Inference*. Ph. D. thesis, Harvard University, Cambridge, Mass.

Louis, A., A. Joshi, and A. Nenkova (2010). Discourse indicators for content selection in summarization. In *Proceedings of the SIGDIAL 2010 Conference*, Tokyo, Japan, pp. 147–156. Association for Computational Linguistics.

Mann, W. C. and S. A. Thompson (1988). Rhetorical structure theory. Toward a functional theory of text organization. *Text 8*(3), 243–281.

Marcu, D. (2000). *The Theory and Practice of Discourse Parsing and Summarization*. Cambridge, MA: MIT Press.

Martin, J. R. (1992). *English text: System and structure*. Benjamins, Amsterdam.

McKeown, K. (1985). *Text Generation : Using discourse strategies and focus constraints to generate natural language text*. Cambridge University Press.

Miltsakaki, E., L. Robaldo, A. Lee, and A. Joshi (2008). Sense annotation in the penn discourse treebank. In *Computational Linguistics and Intelligent Text Processing*, pp. 275–286. Springer.

Mladová, L., S. Zikanova, and E. Hajicová (2008). From sentence to discourse: Building an annotation scheme for discourse based on prague dependency treebank. In *LREC*.

Oza, U., R. Prasad, S. Kolachina, S. Meena, D. M. Sharma and A. Joshi (2009). Experiments with annotating discourse relations in the Hindi Discourse Relation Bank. In *Proceedings of the 7th International Conference on Natural Language Processing (ICON-2 009)*, Hyderabad, India.

Prasad, R., N. Dinesh, A. Lee, E. Miltsakaki, L. Robaldo, A. Joshi, and B. Webber (2008). The Penn Discourse TreeBank 2.0. In *Proceedings of 6th International Conference on Language Resources and Evaluation (LREC2008)*.

Prasad, R., A. Joshi, N. Dinesh, A. Lee, E. Miltsakaki, and B. Webber (2005). The Penn Discourse TreeBank as a resource for natural language generation. In *Proceedings of the Corpus Linguistics Workshop on Using Corpora for NLG*, Birmingham, U.K.

Prasad, R., S. McRoy, N. Frid, A. Joshi, and H. Yu (2011). The biomedical discourse relation bank. *BMC bioinformatics 12*(1), 188.

Prasad, R., B. Webber, and A. Joshi (2014). Reflections on the penn discourse treebank, comparable corpora, and complementary annotation. *Computational Linguistics 40*(4), 921–950.

Redeker, G. (1990). Ideational and pragmatic markers of discourse structure. *Journal of pragmatics 14*(3), 367–381.

Reese, B., P. Denis, N. Asher, J. Baldridge, and J. Hunter (2007). Reference manual for the analysis and annotation of rhetorical structure. Unpublished Ms. http://comp.ling.utexas.edu/discor/.

Sanders, T. J. and M. Scholman (2012). Categories of coherence relations in discourse annotation. Presented at the International Workshop on Discourse Annotation. Utrecht Institute of Linguistics, Universiteit Utrecht.

Sanders, T. J. M., W. P. M. Spooren, and L. G. M. Noordman (1992). Toward a taxonomy of coherence relations. *Discourse Processes 15*, 1–35.

Van Dijk, T. A. (1979). Pragmatic connectives. *Journal of pragmatics 3*(5), 447–456.

Verberne, S., L. Boves, P.-A. Coppen, and N. Osstdijk (2007). Discourse-based answering of why-questions. *Traitement Automatique des Langues, Special Issue on Computational Approaches to Document and Discourse 47*(2), 21–41.

Webber, B., A. Joshi, M. Stone, and A. Knott (2003). Anaphora and discourse structure. *Computational Linguistics 29*(4), 545–587.

Wolf, F. and E. Gibson (2005). Representing discourse coherence: A corpus-based study. *Computational Linguistics 31*(2).

Zhou, Y. and N. Xue (2012). Pdtb-style discourse annotation of chinese text. In *Proceedings of the 50th Annual Meeting of the Association for Computational Linguistics: Long Papers-Volume 1*, pp. 69–77. Association for Computational Linguistics.

Zufferey, S., L. Degand, A. Popescu-Belis, T. Sanders, et al. (2012). Empirical validations of multilingual annotation schemes for discourse relations. In *Eighth Joint ISO-ACL/SIGSEM Workshop on Interoperable Semantic Annotation*, pp. 77–84.

Appendix: Semantics of Annotation Structures

Following the approach to the semantic interpretation of annotation structures outlined in ISO 24617-6 (Principles of semantic annotation), a semantic interpretation of the annotation structures defined by the abstract syntax can be obtained by compositionally interpreting annotation structures through their translation into Discourse Representation Structures (DRSs). The following rules define a translation from entity structures and link structures to DRSs. Discourse referents for the arguments of a discourse relation are paired with the markables of their textual realizations, as proposed by Bunt (2014), in order to make sure that the correct arguments are linked to the discourse relations in which they participate; this is necessary when an annotation structure is interpreted for a text fragment with multiple occurrences of the same discourse relation. The markables can be eliminated when the arguments of a discourse relation have been identified (e.g. merging with clause-internal semantics). In the rules below, a' is the vocabulary item naming the concept a of the conceptual inventory.

1. Relation entity structures: $I(\langle m_i, r_j \rangle) = \begin{array}{|c|}\hline \langle m'_i, r \rangle \\ \hline r'_j(r) \\ \hline \end{array}$

2. Argument entity structures: $I(\langle m_k, t \rangle = \begin{array}{|c|}\hline \langle m'_k, e \rangle \\ \hline t'_j(e) \\ \hline \end{array}$

3. Link structures with explicit discourse relation: $I(\langle \rho, \varepsilon, \alpha \rangle) = \begin{array}{|l|}\hline \langle m'_\rho, r \rangle, \langle m'_\varepsilon, x \rangle \\ \hline \alpha'(r,x) \\ \hline \end{array}$

4. Link structures for implicit discourse relation: $I(\langle r_j, \langle m_1, m_2 \rangle \rangle) = \langle \{r, \langle m'_1, x \rangle, \langle m'_2, y \rangle\}, \{r'_j(r),$ $(\sigma(r_j))'_1(r,x), (\sigma(r_j))'_2(r,y)\}\rangle$ or in box notation: $\begin{array}{|l|}\hline r, \langle m'_1, x \rangle, \langle m'_2, y \rangle \\ \hline r'_j(r) \\ (\sigma(r_j))'_1(r,x) \\ (\sigma(r_j))'_2(r,y) \\ \hline \end{array}$

The following examples illustrate this for (a) an explicit 'semantic' Cause relation and (b) an implicit 'pragmatic' Cause relation.

(7) a. Carl is crazy, because he got his father's bad genes.
    b. Carl is crazy; he beats his wife.

(8) Entity structures and link structures for (7) according to DRelML abstract syntax:
    a. $\langle \{ \langle m_1, \textit{situation} \rangle, \langle m_3, \textit{situation} \rangle, \langle m_2, r_{cause} \rangle \} \} \rangle$
    $\langle \langle m_1, \textit{situation} \rangle, \langle m_2, r_{cause} \rangle, r_{cause-arg2} \rangle$
    $\langle \langle m_3, \textit{situation} \rangle, \langle m_2, r_{cause} \rangle, r_{cause-arg1} \rangle$
    b. $\langle \{ \langle m_1, \langle \textit{dialog-act} \rangle, \langle m_2, \textit{situation} \rangle \} \rangle$
    $\langle r_{cause}, \langle m_1, m_2 \rangle \rangle$

Annotation representations for (8) according to DRelML concrete syntax:

(9) a. See (6b)

    b. [a1] <drArg xml:id="a1" target="#m1" argType="dialogAct"/>
    [a2] <drArg xml:id="s2" target="#m2" argType="situation"/>
    [L1] <implRel xml:id="r1" rel="cause" markables="#m2 #m1" disConn="because"/>

Discourse Representation Structures for (8), after elimination of marbles paired with discourse referents:

(10) a. See (6c)

    b. a1 U a2 U L1 = $\begin{array}{|l|}\hline \text{r, e1, e2} \\ \hline \text{cause(r)} \\ \text{dialogue-act(e1)} \\ \text{result(r,e1)} \\ \text{situation(e2)} \\ \text{reason(r,e2)} \\ \hline \end{array}$

Analysis of Temporal Expressions Annotated in Clinical Notes

Hegler Tissot
Federal University of Parana, Brazil
hctissot@inf.ufpr.br

Angus Roberts
University of Sheffield, UK
angus.roberts@sheffield.ac.uk

Leon Derczynski
University of Sheffield, UK
leon.derczynski@sheffield.ac.uk

Genevieve Gorrell
University of Sheffield, UK
g.gorrell@sheffield.ac.uk

Marcos Didonet Del Fabro
Federal University of Parana, Brazil
marcos.ddf@inf.ufpr.br

Abstract

Annotating the semantics of time in language is important. THYME (Styler et al., 2014) is a recent temporal annotation standard for clinical texts. This paper examines temporal expressions in the first major corpus released under this standard. It investigates where the standard has proven difficult to apply, and gives a series of recommendations regarding temporal annotation in this important domain.

1 Introduction

Time provides a substrate for the human management of perception and action. As a pervasive element of human life, time is a primary element that allows us to observe, describe and reason about what surrounds us in the world (Caselli, 2009). As a cognitive and linguistic component for describing changes which happen through the occurrence of events, processes, and actions, time provides a way to record, order, and measure the duration of such occurrences (Bartak et al., 2013).

Understanding temporal information has become crucial for several language processing applications, such as question answering, text summarisation, information retrieval, and knowledge base population. To this end, it is important to develop strong annotation standards and corpora for temporal semantics. Challenges in developing these standards include: a) how to formally represent the elements that describe temporal concepts; and b) what procedures should be performed by an algorithm, in order to deal with the set of temporal reasoning operations that humans seem to perform relatively easily (Caselli, 2009). The sub-problem of automatic recognition of temporal expressions within natural language text is a particularly challenging and active area in computational linguistics (Pustejovsky et al., 2003).

One way of iteratively improving annotation standards and corpora is to use human annotations to test an annotation model (Pustejovsky and Moszkowicz, 2012). This paper provides an analysis of temporal expression annotation in one such corpus, in an effort to gather information on the underlying model and to improve future annotation efforts.

Our analysis is based on the corpus and standard that backed a recent shared annotation exercise in SemEval (Semantic Evaluation) 2015.[1] SemEval is a series of evaluations that aims to verify the effectivenesses of existing approaches to semantic analysis. SemEval-2015 Task 6, Clinical TempEval (Bethard et al., 2015), was a temporal information extraction task over the clinical domain, using clinical notes and pathology reports, focused on identification of spans and features for time expressions (TIMEX), and based on specific annotation guidelines. Clinical TempEval temporal expression

[1] http://alt.qcri.org/semeval2015/

results[2] were given in terms of Precision, Recall and F1-score for identifying spans and classes of temporal expressions. The identification of expressions should be based on a set of provided guidelines.

The clarity of guidelines, skill of annotators and quality of annotated resource can be estimated by measuring agreement between annotators. It is recommended that the target inter-annotator agreement for linguistic resources be at or above 0.90 (Hovy et al., 2006). Clinical TempEval's timex annotations had an IAA of 0.80 (or 0.79) (Styler et al., 2014), suggesting that these can be improved.

To investigate the quality of the dataset and annotation standard in Clinical TempEval, we have used a rule-based system using JAPE (Cunningham et al., 2011) based as closely as possible on the annotation guidelines, and referring to the corpus for guidance in edge cases. When evaluated using the Clinical TempEval scoring software, this system obtained good Recall (0.795 for timex spans and 0.756 for timex classes) but low precision ranging from 0.29 to 0.49. These results are low compared to the state of the art on other temporally annotated corpora.

In order to discover the reason for the low precision, we analysed the differences between our system and the manually-annotated Clinical TempEval corpus. Our analysis demonstrated how difficult it is to create a manually annotated Gold Standard for time expressions and why this problem is still open in computational linguistics. The analysis is based on a methodology composed of six steps, from manual annotation of the input data, to finding and classifying the time expressions, and finally to a classification of the discrepancies found.

Finally, we make some recommendations that could assist in the production of high quality gold standards. These are: a) improving the annotation guidelines to make rules clearer in terms of what should or should not be annotated; b) expanding the number of examples in the guidelines; c) increasing the number of annotations by the use of an automatic annotation process for those constructs that can be represented by simple, unambiguous rules. This should help avoid the low recall that can sometimes result from a manual annotation process.

This article is organised as follows: Section 2 describes the methodology we used to perform the analysis; Section 3 describes the analysis results and Section 4 gives a series of recommendations in order to guide future temporal annotation in the clinical domain. Section 5 refers to the related work, and Section 6 concludes with final considerations and future work.

2 Methodology

SemEval-2015 Task 6 (Clinical TempEval) was a temporal information extraction task over the clinical domain, using clinical notes and pathology reports for cancer patients provided by Mayo Clinic.[3] Clinical TempEval focuses on identification of: spans and features for timexes, event expressions, and narrative container relations. For time expressions, participants identified expression spans within the text and their corresponding classes: DATE, TIME, DURATION, QUANTIFIER, PREPOSTEXP or SET.[4]

Participating systems had to annotate timexes according to the guidelines for the annotation of times, events and temporal relations in clinical notes – THYME Annotation Guidelines (Styler et al., 2014) –, which is an extension of ISO TimeML (Pustejovsky et al., 2010) developed by the THYME project.[5] Further, ISO TimeML extends two other guidelines: a) TimeML Annotation Guidelines (Sauri et al., 2006), and b) TIDES 2005 Standard for the Annotation of Temporal Expressions (Ferro et al., 2005).

For Clinical TempEval two datasets were provided. The first was a training dataset comprising 293 documents with a total number 3818 annotated time expressions. The second dataset comprised 150 documents with a total of 2078 annotations. This was used for evaluation and was then made available to participants, after evaluations were completed. Each annotation identified the span and class of each timex. Table 1 show the number of annotated timex by class in each dataset.

[2] `http://alt.qcri.org/semeval2015/task6/index.php?id=results`

[3] `http://www.mayoclinic.org`

[4] There was no time normalisation task in Clinical TempEval

[5] `http://thyme.healthnlp.org/`

Table 1: Time expressions per dataset.

Class	Training	Evaluation
DATE	2583	1422
TIME	117	59
DURATION	433	200
SET	218	116
QUANTIFIER	162	109
PREPOSTEXP	305	172
Total	**3818**	**2078**

In order to understand why our system achieved such low Precision in the final Clinical TempEval results, we performed an extensive analysis of the manually annotated time expressions provided for that task, following the steps described below:

- **Manual annotations**: we tabulate all the manually annotated timexes from the Clinical TempEval corpus, listing the timex string, the timex partial sentence (including two previous and following timex tokens), the timex span (begin and end offset boundaries), and the timex class.
- **System result**: we created a similar list with the timexes identified by our system.
- **Matches & Similarities**: we compared the manual annotations with our system result to identify a) those timexes that match in terms of span and class, b) those that are similar in terms of span (at least one overlapping character), and c) those that do not have a corresponding entry.
- **Guideline reference**: For each timex that did not match, we identified the guideline, topic and section corresponding to the inconsistency.
- **Agreements & Disagreements**: we set as an "annotation agreement" each timex that a) had the exact same span and class in both manual annotated corpus and our system result, and b) complied with the annotation guidelines – an "annotation disagreement" happened when one of the previous conditions failed.
- **Found expressions**: We checked in the corpus, using a mixture of word lists and simple patterns, for additional timexes that were neither manually annotated as part of the reference corpus, nor identified by our system. We refer to the combined set of (a) manually annotated expressions, (b) expressions automatically identified by our system, and (c) these additional expressions additionally found, as the "found expressions". We will refer to this combined set of found expressions in Section 3.

Table 2 lists some examples of differences we found between the annotated corpus and automatically created annotations, in terms of timex span and/or class.

Table 2: Examples of differences between the manually annotated corpus, and automatic annotations.

	Manual Annotation		System Result	
Sentence	**Timex**	**Class**	**Timex**	**Class**
12-MAY-2001 21:11	12-MAY-2001	DATE	12-MAY-2001 21:11	TIME
lived 30 years later	30 years	DURATION	30 years later	DATE
for a total of 12 cycles	a total of 12	QUANTIFIER	12 cycles	QUANTIFIER
treated with ten cycles of	ten	QUANTIFIER	ten cycles	QUANTIFIER
hematochezia at that time	at that time	DATE	that time	DATE
he had a MI before 1994	before 1994	DATE	1994	DATE
consists of one beer per day	day	DATE	per day	SET
bleeding for six-months	for six-months	DURATION	six-months	DURATION
postdialysis labs in the morning	in the morning	DATE	the morning	TIME
heart rate of 60 beats per minute	minute	DURATION	per minute	SET
abscess drained in the spring of 2009	spring of 2009	DATE	the spring of 2009	DATE

3 Annotation Analysis

We analysed the annotated datasets provided by Clinical TempEval following the methodology described in Section 2. We considered 4 types of disagreements: a) inconsistency on the annotated span and class; b) non-markable expressions; c) frequent expressions; and d) quantifiers. Each of these is explained below.

3.1 Analysis of Span and Class

When comparing the guidelines against the manually annotated corpus we can observe some inconsistencies concerning the span and the class feature of a timex. We can expect to see a degree of error in any manually annotated corpus; however, we find similar divergences occurring repeatedly. Table 3 summarises all the expression types we analysed, detailing the number of annotation agreements and disagreements, as well as the total number of expressions found in the corpus.

Table 3: Timex class and span inconsistences.

Kind of expression	Annotation Agreements	Annotation Disagreements	Found Expressions
Periods of the day	38	51	107
Temporal granularity as frequency	11	44	80
Explicit times	18	26	445
DATE modified to DURATION	35	60	95
DURATION from explicit DATEs	11	8	19
Total	**113**	**189**	**746**

According to TimeML Annotation Guidelines (section 2.2.3), expressions which refer to a time of the day, should be annotated as a class TIME, even if in a very indefinite way (as periods of the day, e.g., "last night" and "the morning of January 31"). From a total of 107 expressions referring to a period of the day, 89 were annotated in the corpus (more than 80%). However, we observed 51 were not annotated as a TIME, but mainly as a DATE class (less than 50% of total number of found expressions).

THYME Guidelines exemplify in section 4.2.6 that temporal granularities denoting a frequency must be annotated as a SET, for example *"monthly", "weekly", "a day", "per day", "a week", "per minute"*. However, 55% of such expressions were incorrectly annotated as DATE or QUANTIFIER (44 disagreements according to the guidelines).

Explicit times of the day should be annotated as a timex of class TIME (section 2.2.3 of TimeML guideline). This should be the case even if such expressions appear isolated in the text (e.g., *"1:33 pm"*) or within a more complex expression together with a date (e.g., *"04-Oct-2010 09:44"*). Less than 10% of the expressions denoting time were manually annotated. Of these, almost 60% represent annotation disagreements as a timex of class DATE instead of TIME.

Section 4.2.3 of THYME Guidelines state that words like "since", "during" and "until" preceding a timex of class DATE should modify the timex class to DURATION. However, in almost 65% of such modified timexes, we found that this rule was not followed, and that the timex was presented as a DATE.

Additionally, in the same section, one can find that two dates can be used to construct a DURATION timex (e.g., "December 2009 through March 2010"). However, because each one represents a single point in time, they should both be separately annotated as DATE rather than DURATION.

3.2 Non-Markable Expressions

The guidelines are clear about a diverse set of non-markable expressions. The TIDES Guidelines have a specific section (3.2) to describe what should not be annotated as a timex, including prepositions and subordinating conjunctions, specific duration and frequency expressions, and proper names. Table 4 lists time expressions found in the provided corpus that are non-markable expressions according to the guidelines.

Table 4: Non-markable time expressions.

Expression	Annotation Disagreements	Found Expressions
Words "Date/Time"	63	359
Non-quantifiable durations	43	185
Prepositions as triggers	130	1248
Total	**236**	**1792**

There is no reference in the guidelines to annotating the words "Date" and "Time" as a timex when they are not part of a more complex expression, as such isolated words cannot be normalised. In expressions like "Date/Time=Mar 3, 2010", it is expected that "Mar 3, 2010" should be annotated as a DATE, but not the words "Date" and "Time" as time expressions of class DATE and TIME respectively. We found 359 occurrences of such words in 217 different documents, from which 63 of them were incorrectly annotated as DATE and TIME (17.5%).

Non-quantifiable durations are not markable, as they refer to some vague duration (interval) of time, including expressions like "duration", "for a long time", "some time", and "an appropriate amount of time". On the other hand, temporal expressions denoting imprecise amount of time should be annotated as a timex (e.g., *"many days"*, *"few hours"*). We found 185 non-quantifiable duration expressions, from which 43 were incorrectly annotated as a timex with class DURATION (almost 25% of disagreement).

Prepositions which introduce noun phrases are never triggers for time expressions and they can never appear as the syntactic head of an annotated expression. In around 10% of those kind of expressions found in the corpus, time expressions were incorrectly annotated including the head preposition (*"in"*, *"on"*, *"at"*, *"during"*, *"after"*, *"since"*, *"until"*). Some examples include "until July", "on Monday", "in the last year".

3.3 Frequent Expressions

We observed that some expressions tend to appear more often than others in the Clinical TempEval datasets. Most of these are a timex of class SET. A SET is defined (section 4.2.6 of THYME Guidelines) as an expression which comprises a quantifier (optional) and an interval to represent a frequency (mandatory). "Three times weekly", "monthly" and "1/day" are considered as a SET, but not "twice" which is considered as a QUANTIFIER.

We selected a set of the most significant expressions, in terms of the number of occurrences, in order to compare the number of manually annotated expressions against the number of expressions which we found within the text. The expressions were organized in 7 groups:

- Present reference expressions of class DATE *"current(ly)"*, *"recent(ly)"*, *"now"*, *"present(ly)"*;
- Past reference expressions of class DATE *"previous(ly)"*, *"the past"*;
- Explicit years *"2009"*, *"2010"*;
- Precise and imprecise expressions of class DURATION *"24-hour"*, *"2 hours"*, *"six-months"*, *"years"*;
- SETs comprising number of times and frequency *"one-time daily"*, *"two times a day"*, *"twice-a-day"*, *"twice-daily"*, *"three times a day"*, *"four times a day"*;
- SETs comprising only frequencies *"every 6 hours"*, *"every 4 hours"*, *"every evening"*, *"every morning"*, *"every bedtime"*;
- SETs following the pattern "999 /min" – such expressions are part of measurements as in *"Pulse Rate=88 /min"* or *"Resp Rate=16 /min"*.

Table 5 shows how many times each expression was manually annotated and how many times we found it within the corpus (number of found occurrences). Considering all of the selected expressions for this analysis, only 23.3% of such expressions were manually annotated. Considering only SET expressions, the percentage of manually annotated expression is even lower (8.5%).

Table 5: Frequent expressions.

Expression	Manually Annotated	Found Expressions
DATE: present reference	372	836
DATE: past reference	52	117
DATE: explicit years	55	91
DURATION: precise and imprecise	22	114
SET: times and frequency	20	1087
SET: frequency	0	216
SETs: *999 /min*	114	266
Total	**635**	**2727**

3.4 Quantifiers

A special type of timex of class QUANTIFIER was introduced in the THYME Annotation Guidelines. These are used to identify expressions such as "twice", "four times", and "three incidents" which represent the number of occurrences of an EVENT. However, the THYME Guidelines do not make it clear whether or not the words that identify the event itself should be part of the timex span.

In order to understand the way in which QUANTIFIERs and associated EVENTs should be annotated, we examined their occurrence in the Clinical TempEval corpus. We listed all non-numerical words that we found either (a) annotated as part of the QUANTIFIER span or (b) immediately after the QUANTIFIER span. Our reasoning was that these represented the repeated EVENT.

Those 20 most frequent EVENT words found in this way are detailed in Table 6. In the table, we compare the number of manually annotated QUANTIFIERs associated with these EVENTs in the reference corpus, with the number of all QUANTIFIERs that we could find, where they were related to the same kind of EVENT. For example, if the reference corpus included a QUANTIFIER annotation for "twice" in the expression "twice before colonoscopy", then we looked for all occurrences of QUANTIFIER expressions associated with "colonoscopy". Only 11.6% of the QUANTIFIERs that we found were manually annotated in reference the corpus.

Note that the THYME Annotation Guidelines explicitly exclude numeric quantifiers of objects as opposed to events, excluding for example "two units of blood". However, we included those words in our analysis as they were used as a referenced EVENT to annotate QUANTIFIERs in the corpus, usually followed by an expression which identifies frequency (e.g., "1 TABLET by mouth every evening").

4 Recommendations

The analysis given in the previous section has led us to think about the way in which manual temporal expression annotation efforts are conducted. We venture to make a number of recommendations, hoping that these will at least be considered in future manual annotation efforts. We discuss our recommendations below.

Annotation guidelines should clearly state the full set of rules defining what should or should not be annotated, and how. For THYME, the annotators had to piece together several guidelines to figure out what to annotate. This is a potential source of error. Training in the use of multiple sets of guidelines could be considered as an alternative.

Examples are a valuable aid to annotators. Although examples are given in the THYME guidelines, the number could be expanded. In the CLEF Project for example (Roberts et al., 2009), each time an

Table 6: Words related to quantifiers.

Related word	Manually Annotated	Found Expressions
tablet	5	1135
unit	3	117
cycle	51	65
"drinking" words*	44	53
session	4	44
pack	19	29
colonoscopy	4	27
fraction	14	22
treatment	5	16
bowel	8	16
episode	7	11
stool	7	10
beat	5	7
occasion	5	5
Total	**181**	**1557**

* "Drinking" words include "cup", "glass", "beer", "can", "drink", "bottle", and "beverage".

annotator raised a question, and each time persistent differences between annotators were found, new examples were added to the guidelines to re-enforce the point raised.

In creating the THYME gold standard, multiple annotators and an adjudication process were used. A potential source of error with this approach is that where all annotators have a low recall and adjudication focuses only on resolving disputes, the resulting recall can be no greater than the union of the two. This casts doubt on the suitability of inter-annotator kappa agreement (Fleiss et al., 1981) as an indicator of the accuracy of annotation of a corpus.

This last point raises the potential merit of using a high recall rule-based system to prepare a corpus, creating annotations for review by human annotators. Some constructs and guidelines can be represented by simple, unambiguous rules, and where this is the case, the rules will most likely outperform the human annotator in terms of recall. We feel that in such high recall cases, the disadvantage of the approach, that there tends to be a poor correction of missing spans, would be outweighed by the increased number of annotations found.

5 Related Work

TimeML (Pustejovsky et al., 2003) is an expressive language for temporal information annotation, designed to connect the processes of temporal analysis of a text with a representation and formal meaning of time. It is a specification language for event and temporal expressions in natural language text able to capture distinct phenomena in temporal markup, to anchor events to temporally denoting expressions, and to order relative event expressions.

The development of temporal annotation standards and corpora has a long history. Of note is the TimeBank corpus (Pustejovsky et al., 2003), which contains 183 news articles annotated with temporal information, events, times and temporal links between events and times. This corpus was developed in multiple iterations, and prior analyses of the annotated data and the annotation standard aided the evolution of both. For example, Boguraev and Ando (2007) presented an extensive analysis of the TimeBank reference corpus in terms of development support of TimeML-compliant analytics, which helped advance the state of the art in temporal annotation. Indeed, iterative application of an annotation standard and examination of the resulting annotated data are critical steps in the MATTER development cycle, used for construction annotation standards (Pustejovsky, 2006; Pustejovsky and Stubbs, 2012).

Within the previous SemEval evaluation, TempEval-3's Task "A" (UzZaman et al., 2013) examined temporal information extraction and normalisation using the complete set of TimeML temporal relations. Most of the participant systems achieved over 0.70 in Precision and Recall, and best approaches achieved 0.82 and 0.77 for strict F1-score on identifying span and value of timexes. TempEval and TempEval-2 (Verhagen et al., 2009, 2010) also included temporal annotation tasks, of which both were followed by informative analyses of the corpora and participant results (Lee and Katz, 2009; Derczynski, 2013), which led to a better understanding of the task as framed in these exercises.

Other researchers have annotated temporal information in clinical text. For example, the CLEF Project (Roberts et al., 2009) semantically annotated a corpus to assist in the extraction of clinical information from text. It used two different schemas to annotate a) clinical entities and relations between them, and b) time expressions and their temporal relations with the clinical entities in the text. The i2b2 Natural Language Processing Challenge for Clinical Records focused on the temporal relations in clinical narratives, attracting 18 participating teams to analyse discharge summaries, annotating time expressions, events, and relations between them (Sun et al., 2013).

6 Conclusions and Future Work

Adapting annotation of temporal semantics to clinical notes is a significant and challenging task. This paper detailed the results of a principled analysis of expert manual annotations of temporal expressions in the THYME schema over a corpus of clinical notes. Discrepancies between annotations and the guidelines were found in multiple categories. The spans or temporal expressions were not always correct. Ambiguity remained regarding the correct timex class, as happened also in TimeML. Wording in the guidelines was sometimes misinterpreted leading to non-markable timexes being annotated. Finally, as in TimeML, confusion appeared around the annotation of complex SET-type timexes and their quantifiers. This data-driven analysis and its findings should help guide future temporal annotation efforts in the clinical domain.

Acknowledgments

We would like to thank the Mayo Clinic for permission to use the THYME corpus, and CAPES,[6] which is partially financing this work. This work received funding from the European Union's Seventh Framework Programme (grant No. 611233, PHEME). AR, GG and LD are part funded by the National Institute for Health Research (NIHR) Biomedical Research Centre and Dementia Biomedical Research Unit at South London and Maudsley NHS Foundation Trust and King's College London.

References

Bartak, R., R. Morris, and K. Venable (2013). *An Introduction to Constraint-Based Temporal Reasoning*. Synthesis Lectures on Artificial Intelligence and Machine Learning. Morgan & Claypool.

Bethard, S., L. Derczynski, J. Pustejovsky, and M. Verhagen (2015). SemEval-2015 Task 6: Clinical TempEval. In *Proceedings of the 9th International Workshop on Semantic Evaluation (SemEval 2015)*. Association for Computational Linguistics.

Boguraev, B. and R. K. Ando (2007). Effective use of TimeBank for TimeML analysis. In *Annotating, extracting and reasoning about time and events*, pp. 41–58. Springer.

Caselli, T. (2009). *Time, Events and Temporal Relations: an Empirical Model for Temporal Processing of Italian Texts*. Ph. D. thesis, Università di Pisa, Pisa, Italy.

[6]http://www.iie.org/en/programs/capes

Cunningham, H., D. Maynard, K. Bontcheva, V. Tablan, N. Aswani, I. Roberts, G. Gorrell, A. Funk, A. Roberts, D. Damljanovic, T. Heitz, M. A. Greenwood, H. Saggion, J. Petrak, Y. Li, and W. Peters (2011). *Text Processing with GATE (Version 6).* GATE.

Derczynski, L. (2013). *Determining the Types of Temporal Relations in Discourse.* Ph. D. thesis, University of Sheffield.

Ferro, L., L. Gerber, I. Mani, B. Sundheim, and G. Wilson (2005). TIDES 2005 standard for the annotation of temporal expressions. Technical report, The MITRE Corporation.

Fleiss, J. L., B. Levin, and M. C. Paik (1981). The Measurement of Interrater Agreement. pp. 212–236.

Hovy, E., M. Marcus, M. Palmer, L. Ramshaw, and R. Weischedel (2006). Ontonotes: the 90% solution. In *Proceedings of the human language technology conference of the NAACL, Companion Volume: Short Papers*, pp. 57–60. ACL.

Lee, C. M. and G. Katz (2009). Error analysis of the tempeval temporal relation identification task. In *Proceedings of the Workshop on Semantic Evaluations: Recent Achievements and Future Directions*, pp. 138–145. ACL.

Pustejovsky, J. (2006). Unifying linguistic annotations: A TimeML case study. In *Proceedings of Text, Speech, and Dialogue Conference.*

Pustejovsky, J., J. Castano, R. Ingria, R. Saurí, R. Gaizauskas, A. Setzer, and G. Katz (2003). TimeML: Robust specification of event and temporal expressions in text. In *in Fifth International Workshop on Computational Semantics (IWCS-5).*

Pustejovsky, J., P. Hanks, R. Sauri, A. See, R. Gaizauskas, A. Setzer, D. Radev, B. Sundheim, D. Day, L. Ferro, and M. Lazo (2003, March). The TIMEBANK corpus. In *Proceedings of Corpus Linguistics 2003*, Lancaster, pp. 647–656.

Pustejovsky, J., K. Lee, H. Bunt, and L. Romary (2010). ISO-TimeML: An international standard for semantic annotation. In *Proceedings of the Seventh International Conference on Language Resources and Evaluation (LREC'10).* ELRA.

Pustejovsky, J. and J. Moszkowicz (2012). The role of model testing in standards development: The case of ISO-Space. In *LREC*, pp. 3060–3063.

Pustejovsky, J. and A. Stubbs (2012). *Natural language annotation for machine learning.* O'Reilly Media, Inc.

Roberts, A., R. J. Gaizauskas, M. Hepple, G. Demetriou, Y. Guo, I. Roberts, and A. Setzer (2009). Building a semantically annotated corpus of clinical texts. *Journal of Biomedical Informatics 42*(5), 950–966.

Sauri, R., J. Littman, R. Gaizauskas, A. Setzer, and J. Pustejovsky (2006). TimeML Annotation Guidelines, Version 1.2.1.

Styler, W., S. Bethard, S. Finan, M. Palmer, S. Pradhan, P. de Groen, B. Erickson, T. Miller, C. Lin, G. Savova, and J. Pustejovsky (2014). Temporal annotation in the clinical domain. *Transactions of the Association for Computational Linguistics 2*, 143–154.

Sun, W., A. Rumshisky, and O. Uzuner (2013). Evaluating temporal relations in clinical text: 2012 i2b2 Challenge. *J Am Med Inform Assoc 20*(5), 806–813.

UzZaman, N., H. Llorens, L. Derczynski, J. Allen, M. Verhagen, and J. Pustejovsky (2013). SemEval-2013 Task 1: TempEval-3: Evaluating Time Expressions, Events, and Temporal Relations. In *Proceedings of the Seventh International Workshop on Semantic Evaluation (SemEval 2013)*, pp. 1–9. ACL.

Verhagen, M., R. Gaizauskas, F. Schilder, M. Hepple, J. Moszkowicz, and J. Pustejovsky (2009). The TempEval challenge: identifying temporal relations in text. *Language Resources and Evaluation 43*(2), 161–179.

Verhagen, M., R. Sauri, T. Caselli, and J. Pustejovsky (2010). Semeval-2010 task 13: Tempeval-2. In *Proceedings of the 5th International Workshop on Semantic Evaluation*, pp. 57–62. ACL.

Rapid FrameNet annotation of spoken conversation transcripts

Jeremy Trione, Frederic Bechet, Benoit Favre, Alexis Nasr
Aix Marseille University, CNRS, LIF
Marseille, France
firstname.lastname@lif.univ-mrs.fr

Abstract

This paper presents the semantic annotation process of a corpus of spoken conversation transcriptions recorded in the Paris transport authority call-centre. The semantic model used is a FrameNet model developed for the French language. The methodology proposed for the rapid annotation of this corpus is a semi-supervised process where syntactic dependency annotations are used in conjunction with a semantic lexicon in order to generate frame candidates for each turn of a conversation. This first hypotheses generation is followed by a rule-based decision module in charge of filtering and removing ambiguities in the frames generated. These rules are very specific, they don't need to generalize to other examples as the final goal of this study is limited to the annotation of this given corpus, on which a statistical frame parser will finally be trained. This paper describes this methodology and give examples of annotations obtained. A first evaluation of the quality of the corpus obtained is also given on a small gold corpus manually labeled.

1 Introduction

Parsing human-human conversations consists in enriching text transcription with structural and semantic information. Such information include sentence boundaries, syntactic and semantic parse of each sentence, para-semantic traits related to several paralinguistic dimensions (emotion, polarity, behavioral patterns) and finally discourse structure features in order to take into account the interactive nature of a conversation.

The applicative context of this work is the automatic processing of human-human spoken conversations recorded in customer service telephone call centers. The goal of processing such data is to take advantage of cues in order to automatically obtain relevant summaries and reports of such conversations for speech mining applications. These processes are needed because coarse-grained analyses, such as keyword search, are unable to capture relevant meaning and are therefore unable to understand human dialogs.

Performing semantic parsing on spoken transcriptions is a challenging task Coppola et al. (2009). Spoken conversation transcriptions have characteristics that make them very different to process from written text Tur and De Mori (2011).

- non-canonical language: spontaneous speech represents a different level of language than the *canonical* one used in written text such as newspaper articles;
- *noisy messages*: for spoken messages, automatic speech transcription systems make errors, especially when dealing with spontaneous speech;
- relevant and superfluous information: redundancy and digression make conversation messages prone to contain superfluous information that need to be discarded;
- conversation transcripts are not self-sufficient: for spoken messages, even with a perfect transcription, non-lexical information (prosody, voice quality) has to be added to the transcription in order to convey speakers' intention (sentiment, behavior, polarity).

The general process of parsing conversations can be divided into three levels: conversational data pre-processing; syntactic parsing; semantic parsing.

The pre-processing level involves the transcription (automatic or manual) of the spoken content and the segmentation into speakers' turns and sentence-like units.

The syntactic parsing level aims to uncover the word relationships (e.g. word order, constituents) within a sentence and support the semantic layer of the language-processing pipeline. Shallow syntactic processes, including part-of-speech and syntactic chunk tagging, are usually performed in a first stage. One of the key activities described in this paper is the adaptation of a syntactic dependency parser to the processing of spontaneous speech. The syntactic parses obtained are used in the next step for semantic parsing.

The semantic parsing level is the process of producing semantic interpretations from words and other linguistic events that are automatically detected in a text conversation or a speech signal. Many semantic models have been proposed, ranging from formal models encoding *deep* semantic structures to shallow ones considering only the main topic of a document and its main concepts or entities. We use in this study a FrameNet-based approach to semantics that, without needing a full semantic parse of a message, goes further than a simple flat translation of a message into basic concepts: FrameNet-based semantic parsers detect in a sentence the expression of frames and their roles Gildea and Jurafsky (2002). Because frames and roles abstract away from syntactic and lexical variation, FrameNet semantic analysis gives enhanced access to the meaning of texts: of the kind *who does what, and how where and when ?*.

We describe in this paper the rapid semantic annotation of a corpus of human-human conversations recorded in the Paris public authority call-centre, the *RATP-DECODA* corpus presented in Bechet et al. (2012). This corpus is presented in section 2. The methodology followed is a semi-supervised process where syntactic dependency annotations are used in conjunction with a semantic lexicon in order to generate frame candidates for each turn of a conversation. This first hypotheses generation is followed by a rule-based decision module in charge of filtering and removing ambiguities in the frames generated. Section 3 describes the adaptation of syntactic parsing models to the processing of spontaneous speech. Section 4 presents the FrameNet semantic model derived for annotating these call-centre conversations, and finally section 5 reports some evaluation results on a small gold corpus manually annotated.

2 The RATP DECODA corpus

The RATP-DECODA[1] corpus consists of 1514 conversations over the phone recorded at the Paris public transport call center over a period of two days Bechet et al. (2012). The calls are recorded for the caller and the agent, totaling over 74 hours of French-language speech.

The main problem with call-center data is that it often contains a large amount of personal data information, belonging to the clients of the call-center. The conversations collected are very difficult to anonymized, unless large amounts of signal are erased, and therefore the corpus collected can't be distributed toward the scientific community. In the DECODA project we are dealing with the call-center of the Paris transport authority (RATP). This applicative framework is very interesting because it allows us to easily collect large amount of data, from a large range of speakers, with very few personal data. Indeed people hardly introduce themselves while phoning to obtain bus or subway directions, ask for a lost luggage or for information about the traffic. Therefore this kind of data can be anonymized without erasing a lot of signal.

Conversations last 3 minutes on average and usually involve only two speakers but there can be more speakers when an agent calls another service while putting the customer on wait. Each conversation is anonymized, segmented and transcribed. The call center dispenses information and customer services, and the two-day recording period covers a large range of situations such as asking for schedules, directions, fares, lost objects or administrative inquiries.

Because speech that can be found in a call-centre context is highly spontaneous, many speech-specific phenomenon such as disfluencies appear with a high frequency. In the RATP-DECODA corpus the

[1]The RATP-DECODA corpus is available for research at the Ortolang SLDR data repository: http://sldr.org/sldr000847/fr

disfluencies considered correspond to repetitions (e.g. *le le*), discourse markers (e.g. *euh*, *bien*) and false starts (e.g. *bonj-*).

Table 1 displays the amount of disfluencies found in the corpus, according to their types, as well as the most frequent ones. As we can see, discourse markers are by far the most frequent type of disfluencies, occurring in 28% of the speech segments.

disfluency type	# occ.	% of turns	10 most frequent forms
discourse markers	39125	28.2%	[euh] [hein] [ah] [ben] [voila] [bon] [hm] [bah] [hm hm] [coutez]
repetitions	9647	8%	[oui oui] [non non] [c' est c' est] [le le] [de de] [ouais ouais] [je je] [oui oui oui] [non non non] [a a]
false starts	1913	1.1%	[s-] [p-] [l-] [m-] [d-] [v-] [c-] [t-] [b-] [n-]

Table 1: Distribution of disfluencies in the RATP-DECODA corpus

Because of this high level of spontaneity, syntactic models such as Part-Of-Speech models or dependency models that were trained on written text have to be adapted. This semi-supervised annotation method is presented in the next section.

3 Semi-supervised syntactic annotation

It has been shown in Bechet et al. (2014) that a great improvement in tagging and parsing performance can be achieved by adapting models to the specificities of speech transcripts. Disfluencies can be integrated into the models without negative impact on the performance, if some annotated adaptation data is available.

In order to adapt the tagger and parser to the specificities of oral French, we have parsed the RATP-DECODA corpus with the MACAON tagger and dependency parser Nasr et al. (2011) and developed an iterative process consisting in manually correcting errors found in the automatic annotations thanks to a WEB-based interface Bazillon et al. (2012).

This interface allows writing regular expressions on the POS and dependency tags and the lexical forms in order to correct the annotations on the whole RATP-DECODA corpus. Then the parser is retrained with this corrected corpus. When the error rate computed on a development set is considered acceptable, this correction process stops. The resulting corpus, although not perfect, constitutes our training corpus, obtained at a reasonably low price compared to the whole manual annotation process of the corpus. This process is described by figure 1.

The accuracy of the new parser is far above the accuracy of the parser trained on written text (French TreeBank) : from 65.8% to 85.9% for Unlabeled Attachment Score (UAS) and from 58.3% to 83.8% for Labeled Attachment Score (LAS). The performances of the parser can be compared to the performances of a parser for written data despite the fact that the parser has been trained on a partially manually corrected corpus.

Two reasons can explain this result. The first one is that the DECODA corpus has a quite restricted and specific vocabulary and the parser used is quite good at learning lexical affinities. The second one is that the DECODA corpus has a rather simple syntax with utterances generally restricted to simple clauses and less common ambiguities, such as prepositional attachment and coordination, than written texts.

One crucial issue is the amount of manual supervision needed to update the models. If a whole annotation of the corpus is needed, the process will be too costly whatever gain in performance is achieved. We display in 2 the learning curve of the POS tagger, starting from a generic model trained on the French

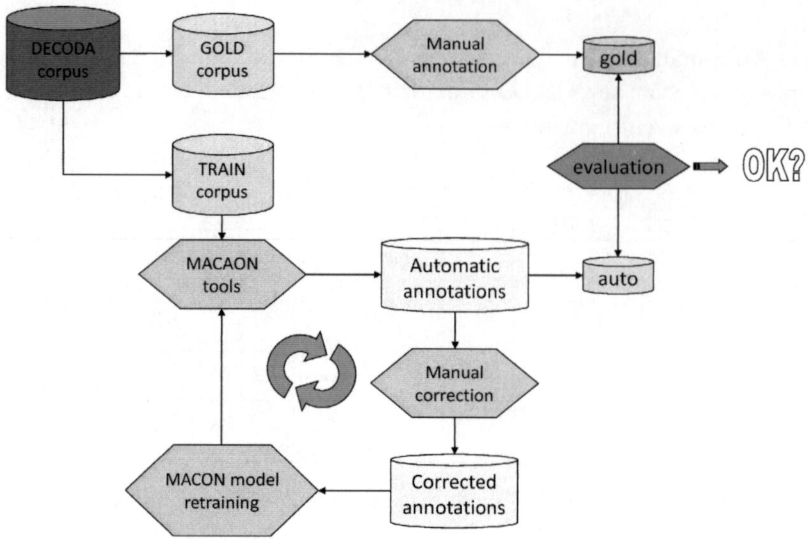

Figure 1: Semi-supervised adaptation process

TreeBank, and including some manual annotation on the target corpus. As we can see, even a very limited annotated subset of the corpus can boost performance: by adding as little as 20 dialogs, the POS error rate drops by more than half (green curve) from 19% to 8%.

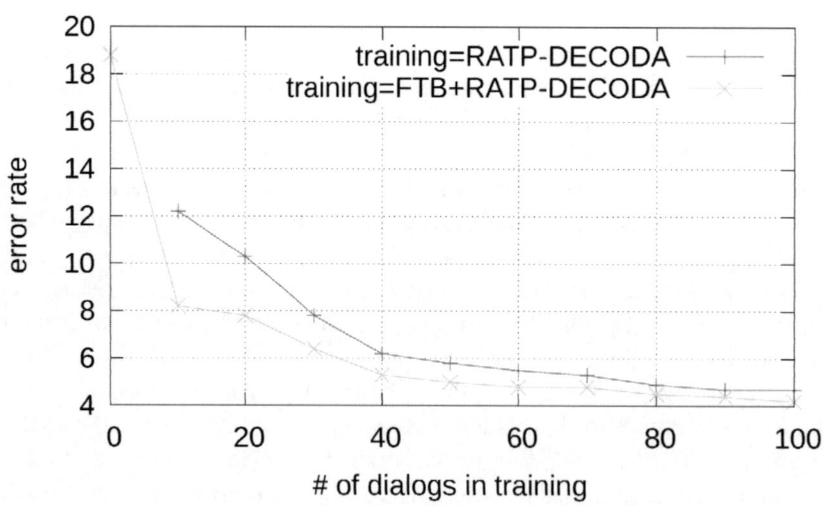

Figure 2: Learning curve of the POS tagger with and without the FTB on the RATP-DECODA corpus

4 From syntactic to semantic annotation

Annotating manually with frame labels a corpus like the RATP-DECODA corpus is very costly. The process we followed in this study is to take advantage of both syntactic annotations and external semantic resources for performing this annotation at a very low cost.

We use in this study a FrameNet model adapted to French through the ASFALDA project. The current model, under construction, is made of 106 frames from 9 domains. Each frame is associated to a set of Lexical Units (LU) that can trigger the occurrence of a frame in a text. The first step, in annotating a corpus with FrameNet, is to detect triggers and generate frame hypotheses for each detection. We did this process on the RATP-DECODA corpus and found 188,231 potential triggers from 94 different frame definitions.

The semi-supervised annotation process presented in this paper consists, for each LU, in searching in the output of the parser for the dependencies (such as subject or object) of each trigger. This first annotation is further refined thanks to semantic constraints on the possible dependent of a given LU, considering the domain of the corpus.

The first step in our annotation process is to select a set of triggers on which frame selection will be applied. In this study we limited our trigger set to the 200 most frequent verbs. By analyzing several triggers on the corpus, we have defined the main domains and frames that we will use to annotate the corpus.

Seven domains were considered:

- Motion.

  Motion frames involve a theme which goes to an area. A vehicle can be use, and several other parameter can be used like the source, the path used, the time, ...
  Most used frames: Motion, Path_shape, Ride_vehicle, Arriving.
  Examples:

Je	voudrais	aller	a Juvisy.
Theme		Motion	Area

I	would like to	go	to Juvisy.
Theme		Motion	Area

- Communication.

  Communication frames involve a communicator sending a message to an addressee. While our corpus is about call center conversation these frame are really important to describe the structure of the call.
  Most used frames: Communication, Request, Communication_response.
  Examples:

je	vous	appelle	parce qu'on m'a redirige vers vous.
Communicator	Addressee	Request	Message

I	call	you	because I was redirected to you.
Communicator	Request	Addressee	Message

- Sentiment expression.

  Sentiment expression frames involve a communicator and an addressee. In our case these sentimental detections can evaluate the behavior of the people in the conversation.
  Most used frames: Judgment_direct_address, Desiring.
  Examples:

je	vous	remercie	beaucoup.
Communicator	Addressee	Judgment_direct_address	Degree

I	thank	you	a lot.
Communicator	Addressee	Judgment_direct_address	Degree

- Commerce.

  Commerce frames involve a buyer, some goods and sometimes a seller. These frames are pretty frequent in every call about tariff or fine paying.
  Most used frames: Commerce_Buy, Commerce_pay.
  Examples:

Vous	devez	acheter	un ticket.
Buyer		Commerce_buy	Goods

You	have	to	buy	a ticket.
Buyer			Commerce_buy	Goods

- Action.

  We call action frames every frames that involve an action linked to a person. These kind of frames are frequent in conversations that deal with misfortune of the caller.
  Most used frames: Losing, Giving, Intentionally_affect.
  Examples:

J'	ai	perdu	mon telephone	dans le bus 38.
Owner		Losing	Possession	Place

I	lost	my phone	in the bus 38.
Owner	Losing	Possession	Place

As mentioned above, all these frames are triggered by the 200 most frequent verbs in the corpus. However, FrameNet was not specially designed for spoken conversations and we had to extend it with two new frames specific to this kind of data:

- Greetings.

  This frame is triggered to represent the opening and the closing of a call. We use the same frame in both cases ("Hello!", "Goodbye!").
  Examples:

Bonjour	monsieur.
Hello	Addressee

Hello	sir.
Hello	Addressee

- Agreement.

  Agreement is a crucial frame in a dialog context. Detecting positive or negative answers to direct Boolean questions in the context of a call-centre dialog is very important. The Agreement frames refer to every mark of agreement ("yes", "of course", ...).
  Examples:

[...]	d'accord	merci.
	Agreement	

[...]	alright	thank you.
	Agreement	

Once this Frame selection process has been done, we are able to produce Frame hypotheses directly from our trigger list of verbs and derive Frame elements from syntactic annotations. There can be only one frame candidate by trigger. If a trigger can correspond to several frames, we use a rule-based approach to choose one frame according to the context. Because the semantic domain of our corpus is rather limited, there are not many ambiguities and most of the verbs only corresponds to one frame, therefore the set of rules needed to remove ambiguities is very limited and restricted to the 5 most frequent verbs (such as *aller - to go*).

To write these rules we selected examples of these ambiguous verbs on our corpus, and wrote rules taking into account the lexical and syntactic context of these verbs. Only six rules were needed, five of them focused on disambiguating motion frames which are the most ambiguous frame in our corpus. Table 2 show an example of rule.

Trigger	Aller	
Rule	Trigger + non verb = motion frame	
Example 1	Un conseiller *va* prendre votre appel.	Not a motion frame
Example 2	Il faut *aller* directement en agence.	Motion frame

Table 2: Example of syntactic rule.

This example illustrates the ambiguity of the trigger verb "*aller*" (*to go*). This verb is very frequent in French, particularly in spontaneous conversations. Similarly to English, this is a polysemic verb that can means "*motion*" as well as an ongoing action (e.g. "*I'm going to do something*"). A simple rule checking if this verb is associated to another verb or to an object can remove this ambiguity (example 1 in 2).

For each rule proposed, we checked on a reference corpus (*gold* corpus presented in the next section) how many ambiguities were correctly resolved, and we kept only the most efficient ones. This process was quite fast as it was done on the Frame hypotheses already produced and checked automatically on a small gold corpus. Just a few iterations allowed us to produce the small set of rules that removed most of the ambiguities of the most frequent verbs.

The Frame selection process consists now, for each trigger in a conversation, to check first if this trigger is ambiguous or not. If it is, a rule should be applied to disambiguate it. If the trigger is not ambiguous, we simply annotate the sentence with the corresponding frame from the dictionary. Due to our very specific corpus, we have a low number of ambiguities and therefore a low number of rules.

5 Evaluation of Frame selection

A small gold corpus was manually defined and annotated. The automatic rule-based Frame selection process is evaluated on this corpus, as presented in figure 1. Our gold corpus is a set on 21 conversations from the RATP-DECODA corpus. These conversations were fully manually annotated by one annotator. The tables below give a representation of the distribution of the frames on this subcorpus, comparing manual annotation and automatic annotation.

Table 3 show us that on average there is at least one trigger per speaker turn. Moreover, we can already tell that the automatic annotation predicts more triggers than the human annotator, and get more variability in the frame chosen. In Table 4 we find our main domain on the RATP-DECODA corpus through the frames. In fact "Hello" and "Judgment_direct_address" represent the structure of the call (opening and closing), while "Request", "Losing", "Motion" and "Commerce_buy" can easily represent the reason of the call.

	Manual annotation	Automatic annotation
Number of Frames per Conversation	23.67	31.33
Number of Frames per speaker turn	0.97	1.24
Number of different frames	26	37

Table 3: Frames distribution on the gold corpus.

Manual Annotation		Automatic annotation	
Frame name	Occurrences	Frame name	Occurrences
Agreement	161	Agreement	216
Hello	95	Hello	95
Judgment_direct_address	59	Motion	45
Motion	33	Communication	34
Request	21	Judgment_direct_address	27
Waiting	20	Desiring	20
Awareness	18	Awareness	19
Communication	15	Intentionally_affect	16
Losing	14	Possibility	12
Commerce_buy	9	Waiting	11

Table 4: Top 10 used frames on the gold corpus.

The quality of the automatic prediction, with respect to the gold corpus, is presented in Table 5. There are different levels of evaluation (trigger selection, frame level, frame element level, span, ...). We chose to evaluate our annotation at the frame level. In other words, we evaluate if a trigger produced the correct frame.

	Recall	Precision	f-measure
Automatic annotation	83.33	94.54	88.58

Table 5: Evaluation on the automatic annotation on the gold corpus.

These first results are satisfying at the precision level is 94.5% of Frame predictions are correct. The recall measure is lower but satisfactory considering that we limited the frame selection process to only the most frequent verbs. A bigger gold corpus is now needed in order to assess the final quality of this corpus.

6 Conclusion

We have presented in this paper a methodology for the rapid annotation of spoken conversation corpus recorded in a French call-centre. This semi-supervised process uses syntactic dependency annotations in conjunction with a FrameNet semantic lexicon. The rule-based decision module in charge of filtering and removing ambiguities in the frames generated is evaluated at each learning cycle on a small manually labelled gold corpus. The first evaluation described in this paper validate this approach by showing good precision scores with an acceptable recall. This corpus will now be used to train a statistical frame parser such as Das et al. (2014) that will be evaluated on other call-centre conversation transcriptions.

References

Bazillon, T., M. Deplano, F. Bechet, A. Nasr, and B. Favre (2012). Syntactic annotation of spontaneous speech: application to call-center conversation data. In *Proceedings of LREC*, Istambul.

Bechet, F., B. Maza, N. Bigouroux, T. Bazillon, M. El-Beze, R. De Mori, and E. Arbillot (2012). Decoda: a call-centre human-human spoken conversation corpus. In *LREC*, pp. 1343–1347.

Bechet, F., A. Nasr, and B. Favre (2014). Adapting dependency parsing to spontaneous speech for open domain spoken language understanding. In *Fifteenth Annual Conference of the International Speech Communication Association*.

Coppola, B., A. Moschitti, and G. Riccardi (2009). Shallow semantic parsing for spoken language understanding. In *Proceedings of Human Language Technologies: The 2009 Annual Conference of the North American Chapter of the Association for Computational Linguistics, Companion Volume: Short Papers*, pp. 85–88. Association for Computational Linguistics.

Das, D., D. Chen, A. F. Martins, N. Schneider, and N. A. Smith (2014). Frame-semantic parsing. *Computational Linguistics 40*(1), 9–56.

Gildea, D. and D. Jurafsky (2002, September). Automatic labeling of semantic roles. *Comput. Linguist. 28*(3), 245–288.

Nasr, A., F. Béchet, J.-F. Rey, B. Favre, and J. Le Roux (2011). Macaon: An nlp tool suite for processing word lattices. In *Proceedings of the 49th Annual Meeting of the Association for Computational Linguistics: Human Language Technologies: Systems Demonstrations*, pp. 86–91. Association for Computational Linguistics.

Tur, G. and R. De Mori (2011). *Spoken language understanding: Systems for extracting semantic information from speech.* John Wiley & Sons.

7 Annex

Abandonment	Accuracy	Activity_pause
Activity_prepare	Activity_resume	Adjusting
Agreement	Agree_or_refuse_to_act	Amalgamation
Arriving	Assessing	Assistance
Attaching	Attempt	Avoiding
Awareness	Becoming	Becoming_a_member
Becoming_aware	Being_in_effect	Being_in_operation
Borrowing	Breaking_apart	Breaking_off
Breathing	Bringing	Building
Bungling	Canceling	Categorization
Causation	Cause_change	Cause_change_of_strength
Cause_harm	Cause_motion	Cause_to_experience
Cause_to_perceive	Certainty	Change_accessibility
Change_event_time	Change_operational_state	Change_position_on_a_scale
Chatting	Choosing	Closure
Coming_to_be	Commerce_buy	Commerce_collect
Commerce_pay	Commerce_sell	Commitment
Communication	Communication_response	Complaining
Compliance	Conferring_benefit	Contacting
Containing	Contingency	Contrition
Control	Cotheme	Deciding
Defending	Departing	Deserving
Desirable_event	Desiring	Difficulty
Duration_description	Duration_relation	Emitting

Emphasizing	Emptying	Erasing
Estimating	Event	Evidence
Existence	Expend_resource	Expensiveness
Experiencer_focus	Experiencer_obj	Explaining_the_facts
Feeling	Filling	Forgiveness
Forming_relationships	Getting	Give_impression
Giving	Givinig	Grasp
Halt	Having_or_lacking_access	Hello
Hiding_objects	Hiring	Impact
Ingestion	Intentionally_affect	Intentionally_create
Judgment	Judgment_direct_address	Justifying
Labeling	Leadership	Lending
Locale_closure	Locating	Location_in_time
Losing	Making_arrangements	Memory
Motion	Name_conferral	Offering
Operating_a_system	Opinion	Participation
Path_shape	Perception_active	Performers_and_roles
Placing	Possession	Possibility
Posture	Practice	Predicting
Preference	Prevarication	Process_continue
Process_end	Processing_materials	Process_start
Questioning	Receiving	Redirecting
Reliance	Removing	rentraire
Repayment	Replacing	Reporting
Request	Required_event	Reserving
Reshaping	Residence	Resolve_problem
Respond_to_proposal	Ride_vehicle	Run_risk
Scrutiny	Self_motion	Self_otion
Sending	Sign	Similarity
Simultaneity	Spelling_and_pronouncing	Statement
Storing	Studying	Subscribing
Success_or_failure	Sufficiency	Surpassing
Taking_sides	Telling	Text_creation
Theft	Topic	Transfer
Trap	Triggering	Using
Using_resource	Verification	Wagering
Waiting	Warning	Work
Working	Negation	

Table 6: Semantic Frames chosen to annotate the RATP-DECODA corpus

Association for Computational Linguistics
209 N. Eighth Street
Stroudsburg, Pennsylvania 18360

CURRAN ASSOCIATES INC
proceedings.com